The Importance of Sentiment in Promoting Reasonableness in Children

Michael S. Pritchard
Emeritus Professor of Philosophy
Western Michigan University

ANTHEM PRESS

Anthem Press
An imprint of Wimbledon Publishing Company
www.anthempress.com

This edition first published in UK and USA 2022
by ANTHEM PRESS
75–76 Blackfriars Road, London SE1 8HA, UK
or PO Box 9779, London SW19 7ZG, UK
and
244 Madison Ave #116, New York, NY 10016, USA

British Library Cataloguing-in-Publication Data
A catalogue record for this book is available from the British Library.

Library of Congress Cataloging-in-Publication Data
A catalog record for this book has been requested.

ISBN-13: 978-1-83998-627-7 (Pbk)
ISBN-10: 1-83998-627-1 (Pbk)

This title is also available as an e-book.

CONTENTS

ACKNOWLEDGMENTS

This book connects my long-standing interest in the philosophical thinking of children with the writings of eighteenth-century Scottish philosophers Thomas Reid, Adam Smith, and David Hume that focus on crucial aspects of the development of children.

My work in this area has been aided by many friends, colleagues, students, and children. I want especially to thank Jacob Castlebury for helping me facilitate an online summer 2021 graduate seminar at Western Michigan University in which students, including Jacob, helpfully commented on the penultimate draft of this book. I also want especially to thank Randall Curren, James Hood, Mary Hood, Karen Mizell, Deborah Mower, Jeff Nielson, Glen Pettigrove, Linda Potter, Alan Preti, Sabine Roesser, Wade Robison, Sally Simmons, Stephen Simmons, Keith Snedegar, Phyllis Vandenberg, and John Wright.

DEDICATION

My greatest thanks go to Elaine Englehardt, who besides holding the title of Distinguished Professor of Ethics at Utah Valley University, is my loving spouse, a frequent collaborator with me, a constant supporter of my efforts on this project and so much else, and is there for me when I need convincing that what I have to say is worth saying. It is to her that I dedicate this book.

PREFACE

More than 25 years ago I argued in *Reasonable Children* that children, as children, can acquire qualities of reasonableness.[1] In doing so, I appealed to children's natural philosophical curiosity. Here I offer further support for this still under-acknowledged view by discussing the writings of three celebrated eighteenth-century Scottish philosophers, Thomas Reid, Adam Smith, and David Hume, as well as sermons by Bishop Joseph Butler, the English predecessor they all admired.

More than 65 years ago I read the following words in my 9th grade world history book: TIME DOES NOT MARCH ON. TIME IS. In large print, with all letters capitalized, these two sentences stood alone, surrounded by empty space. This interruption of the standard pages of historical narrative in small print with occasional pictures and special tables was simply passed over in class as we plodded through the seemingly endless text. However, I still remember silently reflecting on what it could possibly mean. Although about history, it is not a statement one would expect to find in a standard history book. Perhaps something like it could be found in a book on *philosophy* of history.

However, there was no discussion of this unusual statement in my class. This neglect of opportunities for philosophical discussion in pre-college classrooms was standard at the time. (Unfortunately, despite notable exceptions, this is still the case.) Alerted by friends that taking a philosophy course was best delayed until one had taken at least a year's worth of college classes, my formal introduction to philosophy was not until my sophomore year at Alma College (Mich.). I then discovered that I had already been captivated by philosophical questions for some time on my own. This encouraged me for the first time to ignore the large clock on the wall while class was in session. It also led classmate Bob White and me to continue discussing philosophical issues on our way to our next class, Introduction to Economics, which was grounded in the questionable philosophical assumption

---

1 Lawrence, Kansas: University Press of Kansas, 1991.

that human motivation is, in the end, exclusively self-interested. So, these two classes marked the beginning of my long venture into the academic world of philosophy.

Nevertheless, I was not well prepared for a question a friend asked me early in my college teaching career: "Do you think that philosophy is for children as well as adults?" I knew, of course, that children were sometimes mentioned in philosophical discussions, but my friend was asking whether children could, or perhaps should, be encouraged to discuss philosophical issues themselves. Taken by surprise, my immediate response to this question was, "I don't know; I haven't thought about that."

"I haven't thought about that?" "Why not?" I later asked myself? What about my own philosophical reflections as a child? What about my two children, then ages 4 and 7? Had I not been listening to them? What about my other significant area of undergraduate concentration, psychology, including the special interest I had developed in theories of children's learning? Admittedly, the emphasis in my psychology classes was typically on the radical behaviorism of B.F. Skinner, but I spent a fair amount of time reacting critically to its methodological assumptions and its puzzling attempts to avoid relying on anything with a "mentalistic" flavor.

Reflecting further on my friend's question, I was embarrassed by my inability to provide even the beginning of a response at the time. But I was determined not to let matters end there. Fortunately, this incident occurred at about the same time that Matthew Lipman's novel, *Harry Stottlemeier's Discovery*[2] began receiving significant media attention because its use in middle school classrooms in Newark, New Jersey was seeming to have a positive impact on the reading and reasoning skills of students.[3] This novel is one of many that Lipman wrote in which children of all ages are portrayed as engaging meaningfully in philosophical reflection. *Harry*, along with its accompanying, massive manual for guiding philosophical discussions with children, encouraged me to make a serious inquiry into whether philosophy could be a suitable subject for children as well as adults.

I spent the next several years visiting elementary school classes and hosting after-school programs in a small public library to discuss philosophical ideas with children. My first book, *Philosophical Adventures With Children*[4] chronicles my eye-opening experiences during those first few years.

---

2 Institute for the Advancement of Philosophy for Children (IAPC), 1970.

3 See my "Philosophy for Children" (2022), online in the *Stanford Encyclopedia of Philosophy* for a discussion of Lipman and IAPC.

4 University Press of America, 1985 (now out of print).

Although my second book on this topic, *Reasonable Children,* drew some of its support from Thomas Reid's writings on practical ethics, I had yet to become acquainted with contemporary Adam Smith's *Theory of Moral Sentiments* (TMS), whose several editions were composed at the same time he was writing his more celebrated *Wealth of Nations.* Reading TMS led me to compare and contrast Smith's views with those of his good friend David Hume and Hume's notable critic, Reid. The resulting set of reflections in this current book is a revisiting of several major concerns of *Reasonable Children* in light of some of my subsequent work on these three thinkers.

My special focus is on their views about the moral development of children. I regard each of the three, in their differing but sometimes complementary ways, as welcoming the sorts of refinements of sentiments that play a fundamental role in the moral development of children. A key question for these philosophers is how best to characterize relationships between reason and sentiment in that development. I argue that each can be regarded as supporting the general view that the moral development of children can fairly be characterized in terms of the degree to which they are becoming reasonable persons.

As in *Reasonable Children,* the first chapter of this book offers some basic thoughts about what features of persons might qualify them as reasonable, as well as some reflections on the extent to which children can exhibit some, if not all, of these features. Then I turn to the task of determining to what extent each of these three Scots might be called on to support the view that children, as children, should be assisted in moving in this direction.

Chapter 1

REASONABLE CHILDREN?

Following the lead of their English predecessor Joseph Butler, eighteenth-century Scottish philosophers Thomas Reid and Adam Smith identified key elements in the makeup of young children that support the idea that, while still children, they can acquire fundamental features of reasonableness. This book is a revisiting of their accounts, with particular attention given to how their views can support current efforts to promote the philosophical thinking of children.

In contrast to Reid and Smith, both of whom attended carefully to Butler's earlier writings on resentment and forgiveness, David Hume did not discuss these reflections. This is so despite his admiration of Butler's work and his familiarity with the writings of his two contemporaries. However, Glen Pettigrove, the current occupant of Glasgow University's Chair of Moral Philosophy (the position once held by Smith, and then by Reid, his immediate successor), offers an account of eighteenth-century Scotland's regard for *meekness* as a virtue that might shed some light on why Hume took a different path. Pettigrove's "Meekness and 'Moral' Anger" (*Ethics*, January 2012) discusses in detail how meekness was standardly regarded as a moral virtue in eighteenth-century Scotland. Among those Pettigrove credits with sharing this assessment of meekness was David Hume.

Today meekness is commonly regarded as a sign of weakness and moral submissiveness. However, Hume and his contemporaries understood it as exhibiting moral strength and anything but submissiveness. In his essay "Of the Standard of Taste," Hume lists meekness, equity, justice, temperance, and charity as concepts that "must always be taken in a good sense."[1] In his *Treatise*, Hume says that meekness is a virtue whose "tendency to the good of society no one can doubt of."[2]

What was this earlier understanding of meekness? A particularly noteworthy mark of its strength was the disposition to resist becoming angry while at the

---

1 In Hume, David. *Four Dissertations,*1757.
2 Bk. 3, pt. 3, sec. 1, par. 1.

same time maintaining firm commitment to moral principle, including support for rules of justice. Pettigrove points out that it was typically contrasted with anger, resentment, wrath, rage, revenge, cruelty, and a persecuting spirit. Credited with constraining anger and related emotions, the meek individual is "slow to anger and is not prone to resent others, to desire their suffering, or to take pleasure in their distress."[3] Pettigrove adds, even when angered, the meek do not sustain their anger long, and they choose enduring evil over trying to overcome evil with evil. He summarizes: "Agent M manifests the virtue of meekness when he or she characteristically responds in a calm and kindly fashion to aggravating treatment" (345).

A message for today, Pettigrove suggests, is that many of us might well try to nurture a "suitably qualified" disposition of meekness in ourselves and in our children (346). He does not elaborate, but this is an important point. Equally important, he adds that "acting virtuously is commonly something we must learn and in which we must be trained" (368). This raises the critical question of just what sort of training is required, a question addressed by Reid and Smith, but slighted by Hume.

Pettigrove observes: "Some of the most dearly loved and widely admired figures in history have been distinguished by their meekness: Socrates, Buddha, Jesus, Abraham Lincoln, Mahatma Gandhi, Martin Luther King, Jr., Nelson Mandela, and the Dalai Lama are each esteemed for manifesting this trait of character" (349). Each exhibited benevolent concern for others despite how badly they and their followers were treated, but they were anything but submissive when being wronged (351–52). They objected to the injustices around them, but they advocated only nonviolent means of registering their protests. Both their recognition of injustice and their non-submissive ways of opposing these wrongs require the engagement of reason and sentiment.

Obviously, the self-command exhibited by the meek is not present in infancy. As Reid and Smith emphasize, self-command is gradually acquired as one's rationality develops. Thus, this rationality is of a practical sort, blending reason and affect in its management of the sentiments. Insofar as the virtue of meekness emerges, it would seem to be a result of this same process. But the training this involves begins only as children are developing their rational powers and the self-discipline these powers can bring with them. Presumably, Hume could have attempted a detailed account of how meekness can emerge from this process, but he did not choose to do so. In such an account, reason would have to play as significant a role as

---

3 Pettigrove, p. 344. Further page references will be noted in the text within parentheses.

sentiment—an observation confirmed by Butler, Smith, and Reid in their critical reflections on resentment. Unfortunately, although all three might well have regarded meekness as a virtue, none of them explicitly discussed this in any detail.

If Hume's appeal to meekness was, in effect, his answer to Butler's critique of resentment and forgiveness, this should place character development in a preeminent position in his view of the moral development of children. Had Hume indicated this, he might well have contributed to recent programs in character education that have made inroads in many pre-college curricula, especially in the United States.

Today's character education advocates commonly hold that there are some basic virtues that are essential for responsible citizenship in a democratic society and that it is the business of schools to help students appreciate their importance. Their view is that, despite sometimes deep moral and religious differences among us, there is also widespread consensus that there is a set of virtues that cuts across these differences.

However, *reasonableness*, often overlooked in this context, is needed to help moderate the virtues and their relationships to one another. Consider, for example, "the six pillars of character" listed in the popular Character Counts movement. As expected, honesty is on its list. But there are occasions in which most would maintain that not being honest is appropriate (e.g., lying to a would-be murderer that one does not know the whereabouts of the innocent person being sought). In short, honesty is not the only virtue, which means that it, too, may need to be subjected to reasonable constraints.

So, as I did in *Reasonable Children* (1996), I first offer some reflections on reasonableness. However, I also offer a word of caution. No concise definition of "reasonableness" will be offered. It might be thought that to get a better grip on what counts as reasonableness, one should seek a definition of this somewhat elusive concept. But here it is advisable to heed the advice of Thomas Reid[4]:

> It is well known, that there are many things perfectly understood, and of which we have clear and distinct conceptions, which cannot be logically defined. No man ever attempted to define magnitude; yet there is no word whose meaning is more distinctly or more generally understood. We cannot give a logical definition of thought, of duration, of number, or of motion.

---

4 Thomas Reid, *Essays on the Active Powers of Man*, pp. 7–8. First published in 1788, but subsequently edited by Knud Haakonessen and James A. Harris (Edinburgh University Press, 2010). Hereafter, this book will be referred to as AP.

When men attempt to define such things, they give no light. They may give a synonymous word or phrase, but it will probably be a worse for a better. If they will define, the definition will either be grounded upon a hypothesis, or it will darken the subject rather than throw light upon it.

If by "logically define" Reid means identifying the necessary and sufficient conditions for the correct use of the term, it is likely right to say that attempting such a definition of "reasonableness" is asking for trouble (or darkness). However, it is also likely right to deny that this idea is "perfectly understood." So, it seems sensible to seek some clarification of the term, but to settle for something other than a "logical definition."

In doing so, the focus will be mainly on how appraisals of reasonableness might be applied to persons, their beliefs, attitudes, actions, and decisions. Appraisals could also be made of policies, practices, and the processes of deliberative bodies (e.g., juries, hospital ethics committees, and research review committees). But even in such settings, the focus here will be mainly on appraisals of the reasonableness (and unreasonableness) of individual persons.

It is important to realize that, although intimately related, reasonableness and rationality are not the same. Individuals can be unreasonable by insisting on getting more than their fair share, but this does not necessarily mean that they are not being rational, even when they are acting at the expense of others. Or individuals might deliberately ignore or suppress evidence contrary to their favored views, be unwilling to reason with others about an issue, or refuse even to listen to others' points of view, without being irrational. In doing this, they will employ some of their rational abilities. But we may rightly assess such behavior as unreasonable.

However, reasonableness is a kind of rationality. It typically emphasizes the importance of having good reasons in support of one's beliefs. Furthermore, these reasons are intended to be capable of standing up to public examination, rather than as simply reflecting one's private ruminations. Finally, even if sometimes it can be rational to be unreasonable, this need not stand in the way of it being rational to be reasonable in such circumstances as well. For example, in response to Crito's attempt to convince Socrates that it would be irrational for him to refuse his friends' offer to help him to escape his imprisonment and thereby avoid his death sentence, Socrates insisted on using standards of reasonableness in deciding whether to accept this offer.[5] Thus, he was prepared

---

5 See "Crito" in Plato, 1981. *Five Dialogues*. Trans. by G. M. A. Grube (Indianapolis: Hackett Publishers).

to opt for the most reasonable choice, even if rationality would not necessarily require this. At the same time, Socrates was convinced that his choice to drink the fatal hemlock instead of escaping with his friends was both reasonable and rational.

The notion of reasonableness being advanced here is meant to be moral in its import. So, it should be thought of in terms of certain *social* features. Especially to be emphasized in the moral development of children is a willingness to think *with* others rather than simply alone. Typically, rationality displays some ability to engage in skillful reasoning. However, Laurence Splitter and Ann Sharp emphasize that reasonableness includes much more[6]:

> Reasonableness is primarily a social disposition: the reasonable person respects others and is prepared to take into account their views and their feelings, to the extent of changing her own mind about issues of significance, and consciously allowing her own perspective to be changed by others. She is, in other words, *willing to be reasoned with.*

In a classroom setting, this sort of active interchange among students promotes what Splitter and Sharp call a *community of inquiry.*[7]

In an earlier account, W. M. Sibley usefully distinguishes "reasonable" in its moral sense from the broader notion of "rational."[8] Insofar as I am rational, he maintains, I may be willing to consider all factors relevant to my circumstances, including likely consequences for others. But, he adds, considering how one's own interests might affect others does not necessarily include regarding the interests of others as important in their own right. This is required if one is "reasonable" in its moral sense.

---

6 Laurence J. Splitter and Ann M. Sharp, *Teaching Better Thinking: The Classroom Community of Inquiry* (Melbourne: Australian Center for Educational Research, 1995), p. 6. [Emphasis added.]

7 In addition to *Teaching Better Thinking: The Classroom Community of Inquiry*, see Ann M. Sharp, "The Community of Inquiry: Education for Democracy," *Thinking*, 9.2 (1991), 31–37 and John C. Thomas, "The Development of Reasoning in Children Through Community of Inquiry," in Ronald Reed and Ann M. Sharp, eds., *Studies in Philosophy for Children: Harry Stottlemeier's Discovery* (Philadelphia: Temple University Press, 1992), 96–104. For more recent considerations of Sharp's views, see Maughn Gregory and Megan Laverty, eds., *Community of Inquiry with Ann Margaret Sharp* (New York; Routledge, 2019).

8 W.M. Sibley, "The Rational versus the Reasonable," *Philosophical Review*, 62, 1953, 557.

Sibley acknowledges that in a nonmoral context being rational and being reasonable may not be significantly different. Someone's investment may turn out badly, but we might agree that reasonable precautions were taken. In such cases, "rational" and "reasonable" both basically mean "prudent."

However, reasonableness in its *moral* sense involves additional features, Sibley points out[9]:

> If I desire that my conduct shall be deemed *reasonable* by someone taking the standpoint of moral judgment, I must exhibit something more than mere rationality or intelligence. To be reasonable here is to see the matter—as we commonly put it—from the other person's point of view, to discover how each will be affected by the possible alternative actions; and, moreover, not merely to "see" this (for any merely prudent person would do as much) but also to be prepared to be disinterestedly *influenced*, in reaching a decision, by the estimate of these possible results. I must justify my conduct in terms of some principle capable of being appealed to by all parties concerned, some principle from which we can reason in common.

As we shall see, Reid and Smith appeal to something very like Sibley's notion of reasonableness in morality. It is perhaps less clear what Hume's stance is; but he, too, rests morality on a general principle in which he tries to ground justice and other moral principles (such as benevolence).

For Sibley, a morally reasonable person is responsive to the perspectives of others, which minimally involves working at understanding what those perspectives are, noting both significant differences from and similarities to one's own. This requires an ability to overcome one's egocentric tendencies to assume that others think and value as we do. Still, having such an ability to some extent does not eliminate the lifelong struggle that all of us have in dealing with residual egocentric tendencies. Furthermore, like-mindedness is not a requirement of reasonableness. The ability to accept, or at least tolerate, differences that are supported with good reasons is itself a mark of reasonableness.[10]

---

9 Ibid.

10 This is a central theme of Bernard Gert's *Common Morality* (Oxford, 2004), which convincingly shows that much of our common morality supports reasonable moral disagreement. Although Gert does not mention Lipman, Sharp, or Splitter's account of reasonableness, it seems clear that all of them defend the notion that differences that are supported with good reasons can all be reasonable.

It is important not to confuse the possibility of reasonable disagreement on some occasions with a general skepticism about the truth of our judgments. Although people may reasonably disagree about many matters, it does not follow that none of the conflicting views are true (or that all of them are "true," each in their own subjective way). Nor does it follow that no views are *un*reasonable. Rather, the point is only that it can be difficult to determine what should count as the best final judgment if, indeed, there is one to be had. (This can be compared with trying to determine, for example, who is the best baseball player. Some can be easily eliminated. But there will still be many from whom to choose, and a diverse set of criteria available for consideration.)

What marks of reasonableness might we look for in children?[11] Prominent features include an ability and disposition to seek relevant information, to listen and respond thoughtfully to others, to be open to new ideas, to give good reasons for one's views, to acknowledge mistakes and misunderstandings, and to display a willingness to compromise (without compromising personal integrity).[12]

Equally important are items that should *not* be on such a list. We should not expect children, insofar as they are reasonable, to feel a need always to agree with others, to be willing to change virtually any belief or conviction, however deeply held, to insist that they are necessarily right and others wrong, or to insist on having their own way.

These considerations provide a rough picture of the sorts of dispositions and tendencies that characterize reasonable people. Furthermore, they also provide an outline of those qualities the schools might hope to encourage in students as they move from childhood toward adulthood.

Of course, reasonableness and unreasonableness are not our only terms of appraisal, and reasonableness cannot stand alone as a value. Our values have many different sources, and there is great diversity among them, both among different persons and within the same person. Not all values are specifically moral values, and there is no reason to insist on uniformity among persons. But even within morality, there may be many different ways of satisfying plausible criteria for being a well-developed, moral person; reasonable people might even disagree about some of the criteria. Nevertheless, the range of possibilities is not limitless. It is important to recognize and be supportive of the earliest appearance of those cognitive and affective capacities that are

---

11 This paragraph, as well as the one that follows it, is based on p. 11 of *Reasonable Children*.
12 See Martin Benjamin, *Splitting the Difference: Compromise and Integrity in Ethics and Politics* (Lawrence, KS: University Press of Kansas, 1991) for an excellent discussion of the importance of compromise while retaining one's integrity.

essential to the development of moral agents; whatever else is emphasized, those capacities that contribute to reasonableness need special attention.

In chapters that follow, readers are invited to assess Reid, Smith, and Hume in regard to how well they articulate their views of children in regard to their readiness to exhibit qualities of reasonableness such as those mentioned above, as well as how children's readiness for philosophical reflection contributes to this.

Chapter 2

THOMAS REID ON THE "SEEDS OF MORALITY"[1]

A central theme in Thomas Reid's *Essays on the Active Powers of Man* (1788) is that, since we are not born with moral sensitivities or dispositions, an account of their development is in order.[2] For Reid, a key factor that enables moral sensitivities to make an early entrance is the young child's ability to communicate sentiments with others. Reid astutely observes that "[...] we can perceive some communication of sentiments between the nurse and her nursling, before it is a month old"[3] (AP, 333). This communication occurs near the beginning of a path from which slowly emerges what Reid calls a person's conscience, a moral sense that guides one's moral attitudes, beliefs, and actions—as well as enable moral exchanges with others.[4]

Thus, for Reid, a child's communication with others has a very early beginning. When morally tinged communication begins is uncertain, but this also is early. Although many of our first moral beliefs and dispositions have strong staying power throughout one's life, this does not imply that we must have also accepted some overriding moral theory, consciously or otherwise, to serve as a grounding for those beliefs and dispositions. Nor, Reid thinks, is the absence of such a theory in itself a moral shortcoming.

---

1 This chapter is a revised version of my earlier "Thomas Reid on the 'Seeds of Morality'," in *The Journal of Scottish Thought*, Vol. 4, 2011, 1–15.

2 Page references in this chapter will be to the 2010 version of *Active Powers* (AP) edited by Knud Haakonessen and James A. Harris (Edinburgh University Press).

3 Attentive father of his own children, Reid may have had an observational advantage over Adam Smith and David Hume, who had no children.

4 Subsequent research confirms that shortly after birth infants respond differently to the sounds of authentic cries of babies as distinct from recordings of such cries. Martin Hoffman (*Empathy and Moral Development*, Barnes & Noble, 2000), e.g., discusses such research in developing his account of empathy in moral development. Further insightful research on the social life of infants and young children is analyzed in psychologist and philosopher Alison Gopnik's *The Scientist in the Crib* (1999) and *The Philosophical Baby* (2012). See, also, *The Moral Life of Babies* (2013) by psychologist and cognitive scientist Paul Bloom.

Reid's discussion of the moral development of children is an extension of his view that morality is for everyone. By attending to the developmental process children go through, he focuses on the essential roles of both reason and sentiment in morality and their deep roots in our natural constitution. As Reid's discussion of moral judgment makes clear, reason and sentiment work together in moral agents whose "seeds of moral discernment" need careful cultivation and nurturing. Finally, attending to this developmental process helps Reid explain why he holds that theories of morality need to defer to practical, common sense when the latter is threatened by the former.

Reid makes a distinction between a "theory of morals" and a "system of morals." The first attempts to provide "a just account of the structure of our moral powers; that is, of those powers of the mind by which we have our moral conceptions, and distinguish right from wrong in human actions" (AP, 282). This is as difficult an area of philosophical inquiry as any, he says. Although this subject is *about* morality, Reid holds that it is of little practical use for everyday moral life. Such a theory "has little connection with the knowledge of our duty; and those who differ most in the theory of our moral powers, agree in the practical rules of morals which they dictate" (AP, 282–283).

Just as we should not expect our vision to improve simply because of what we learn about how the eye operates, we should not expect our moral judgment to improve by having a good "theory of morals" (AP, 283). This may seem to underestimate the practical significance of theories of vision, especially in light of the practical improvements that have come from eyeglasses and other practical visual aids that make use of such theories. However, Reid could reply that, yes, such practical aids do result from technological innovations that rely on theories of vision; but the *users* of such devices do not need to understand these theories in order to experience improved vision. In the case of eyeglasses, for example, all the user need do is undergo an eye test (much of which one need not understand), get a prescription for the lens (which one need not understand), order the eyeglasses, and then wear them. If the ophthalmologist who makes use of theories of vision is competent, the result should be improved vision for the user. This is what happened to me when I acquired my first pair of eyeglasses at age five. The ophthalmological perspective that informed the prescription for these eyeglasses, however, was not mine; nor did I understand the underlying theory of vision that was employed on my behalf.

In the aesthetic realm, Reid says: "In order to acquire a good eye or a good ear in the arts that require them, the theory of vision and the theory of sound, are by no means necessary, and indeed of very little use. Of as little necessity or use [for us, as moral agents] is what we call the theory of morals, in order to improve our moral judgment" (AP, 283). Important as theories of morals may be for the philosophy of the human mind, says Reid, they should not be regarded as a part of practical systems of morals that are embraced and used by moral agents.

This second subject, "systems of morals," is *within* everyday practical morality and can be put to practical use by reminding us of, and helping us sort out, what should matter most to us. However, says Reid, these two subjects are usually discussed together, often resulting in needless and dangerous confusion. When this happens, it is Reid's view that it is the "theory of morals" that should give way, not practical morality:

> For there cannot be better evidence, that a theory of morals [...] is false, than when it subverts the practical rules of morals. (AP, 322)

However, if it is borne in mind that theories of morals and systems of morals are distinct subjects, Reid thinks we will see that ordinary persons are quite capable of understanding what morality commonly requires of us without relying on a theory of morals. This is fundamental to practical morality because, Reid says: "Moral conduct is the business of every man; and therefore the knowledge of it ought to be within the reach of all" (AP, 185). So, Reid issues a warning:

> By the name we give to it [the theory of morals], and by the custom of making it a part of every system of morals, men may be led into this gross mistake, which I wish to obviate, that in order to understand his duty, a man must needs be a philosopher and a metaphysician. (AP, 283)

In illustrating what he has in mind, Reid directs our attention to children, offering the following example:

> One boy has a top, another a scourge; says the first to the other, "If you will lend me your scourge as long as I can keep up my top with it, you shall next have the top as long as you can keep it up." "Agreed," says the other. This is a contract perfectly understood by both parties, though they never heard of the definition given by Ulpian or by Titius. And each of them knows, that he is injured if the other breaks the bargain, and that he does wrong if he breaks it himself. (AP, 329)

This passage is typical of Reid's reflections on practical morality in his *Active Powers of Man*. What may seem unusual to us today is the extent to which Reid, as a philosopher, is interested in exploring the moral development of children, from infancy onward. It is much more common for philosophers, then and now, to focus primarily on adults, who presumably are already far down the road of moral development, perhaps as fully developed morally as they ever will be.

This is as it should be, it might be thought. On the one hand, if we are trying to develop a defensible account of practical morality, isn't it appropriate to concentrate on those whose moral capacities are reasonably well developed and to whom moral questions can meaningfully be addressed? They— not rocks, trees, squirrels, or even foxes—are the subjects whose moral sensibilities need to be understood and taken into account. Perhaps only the philosophically inclined have a serious and abiding interest in questions pertaining to a "theory of morals."[5] However, adult moral agents can seriously entertain at least some basic questions about morality without being philosophers or metaphysicians—just as we can address and solve mathematical problems without being mathematicians.

On the other hand, if we are trying to articulate a "system of morals," the views of ordinary adults, not just philosophers, should be taken seriously. Ordinary adults have experience in navigating their way through at least significant parts of "moral systems," and they occasionally puzzle more generally over questions about how they should live their lives, and why. However, it might be thought that children need not be taken seriously in this way. They are too young and inexperienced. Of course, children do matter. After all, they are in the care of adults for a significant part of their lives. Eventually, they will become adults and, thus, join those who are capable of reflecting on these questions.

But what if the voices of children are given a hearing, just as those of adults are? Philosopher Gareth Matthews offers this example:[6]

> IAN (six years) found to his chagrin that the three children of his parents' friends monopolized the television; they kept him from watching his favorite program. "Mother," he asked in frustration, "why is it better for three people to be selfish than for one?"

---

5 Late nineteenth-century philosopher Henry Sidgwick might be thought to be such a thinker. His *Methods of Ethics* argues at great length that utilitarianism grounds morality. However, in his *Practical Ethics* he discusses the desirability of thoughtful non-theorists meeting with each other to try to resolve pressing practical issues of the day without getting bogged down in trying to "get to the bottom of things"—a quest that he thought would only extend disagreement. Better, he thought, to settle on readily available points of agreement that all plausible grand theories accept. On this, see my "Sidgwick's *Practical Ethics*," in *International Journal of Applied Philosophy*, 12:2, 1998, pp. 147–151.

6 *Philosophy and the Young Child*, Harvard, 1980, 28.

Matthews regarded Ian's question as posing a worthy challenge to utilitarian thinking. Can children as young as Ian reflect meaningfully on such questions? Matthews invited a group of 8–10 year olds to consider Ian's question. What followed was a rather sophisticated discussion of fairness and rights. For the most part, these children resisted the use of utilitarian thinking in this case.[7] This does not mean that they could not understand utilitarian thinking. Rather, they objected to its use in this kind of situation.

Many may find it surprising that moral reflection at this level can be undertaken by children at such a young age; but if we doubt that it can, perhaps we should wonder how (or even whether) children will be able to do this once they are adults.[8] They will have "grown up," we might say. But from where? What do they *bring with them* that enables them to do what adults can do? Their lives begin in infancy before they have any moral notions at all; but by the time they are adults they are filled with them. What has happened?

Reid is interested in such questions of moral development in part, it seems, because answering them can help us better understand what morality in practice can be, what its practical basis is, and what its importance is in everyday life. In focusing on these questions, Reid often employs botanical metaphors—frequently referring to, for example, "the seeds of morality" and "the seeds of moral discernment." This opens two avenues for exploration. The first compares and contrasts human beings as moral agents with animals ("brutes") that, we presume, lack the appropriate "seeds," rendering them, therefore, incapable of becoming moral agents. The second requires us directly to attend to questions of moral development—children who are presumably on enroute to becoming adults eventually.

Turning to the first, Reid notes that a human being is influenced by a *"great number of active principles:"*

His body, by which his mind is greatly affected, being a part of the material system, is subject to all the laws of inanimate matter. During some part of his existence, his state is very like that of a vegetable. He rises, by imperceptible degrees, to the animal, and, at last, to the rational life, and has the principles that belong to all. (AP, 76)

Noteworthy is Reid's presumption that, even though we eventually develop our rational capacities, we do not thereby abandon our animal principles.

---

7 *Dialogues With Children*, Harvard, 1984.
8 Ch. 6, "Conversations and Critical Thinking," will provided an extended illustration of the ability of 10–11 year olds to engage in nuanced reflection on the morality of a variety of kinds of reciprocal relations in everyday situations.

They still must be acknowledged; in fact, they must somehow be brought within the scope of self-government, which requires the use of rational powers. But, Reid holds, the story is not the same for animals ("brutes"). They seem incapable of moving significantly into a life involving the use of reason—and, unlike humans, their flourishing does not require this.

The appetite of animals, says Reid, may be restrained by a stronger principle, but not by a *moral* one:

> A dog, when he is hungry, and has meat set before him, may be kept from touching it by the fear of immediate punishment. In this case, his fear operates more strongly than his desire. (AP, 97)

This, Reid says, does not incline us to ascribe any moral virtue to the dog:

> The animal is carried by the strongest moving force. This requires no exertion, no self-government, but passively to yield to the strongest impulse. This, I think, brutes always do; therefore we attribute to them neither virtue nor vice. We consider them as being neither objects of moral approbation nor disapprobation. (AP, 97)

As far as we can tell, says Reid, nonhuman animals ("brutes") are incapable of self-government.[9] For example, they are incapable of promising, which requires not only having a conception of promising but also having a sense of past, present, and future that enables them to make and keep commitments.

Reid makes no attempt to determine precisely when children are capable of making promises and may be held accountable for keeping or breaking them. We do not know how old Reid imagines the boys playing with a top and scourge are. There is no need to assume that their rational powers are fully formed; but these powers are developing—gradually, and by degree.

At some point (Reid does not speculate about just when this might occur) we acquire a notion of what is "our good on the whole":

> It will not be denied that man, when he comes to years of understanding, is led by his rational nature, to form the conception of what is good for him upon the whole.

---

9 Contemporary students of nonhuman life may question the clean lines Reid draws between humans and nonhumans. But there does not seem to be any reason to suppose that Reid could not adjust his views in light of empirical evidence, which at the time he thought confirmed his views.

How early in life this general notion of good enters into the mind, I cannot pretend to determine. It is one of the most general and abstract notions we form.

Whatever makes a man more happy, or more perfect, is good, and is an object of desire as soon as we are capable of forming the conception of it. The contrary is ill, and is an object of aversion.

In the first part of life we have many enjoyments of various kinds; but very similar to those of brute-animals.

They consist in the exercise of our senses and powers of motion, the gratification of our appetites, and the exertions of our kind affections. These are chequered with many evils of pain, and fear, and disappointment, and sympathy with the suffering of others. (AP, 154)

For animals and very young children, the focus is largely on the present. ["The present object, which is most attractive, or excites the strongest desire, determines the choice, whatever be its consequences" (AP, 154).] However:

As we grow up to understanding, we extend our view both forward and backward. We reflect upon what is past, and, by the *lamp of experience*, discern what will probably happen in time to come [...].

We learn to observe the connexions of things, and the consequences of our actions; and taking an extended view of our existence, past, present, and future, we correct our first notions of good and ill, and form the conception of what is good or ill upon the whole; which must be estimated, not from the present feeling, or from the present animal desire or aversion, but from a due consideration of its consequences, certain or probable, during the whole of our existence. (AP, 155)

Reid sees a very close relationship between having an adequate conception of our good on the whole and grasping the demands of morality, both of which require the development of appropriate rational powers and an appreciation of our natural social affections:

[...] this principle leads directly to the virtues of prudence, temperance, and fortitude. And, when we consider ourselves as social creatures, whose happiness or misery is very much connected with that of our fellow-men; when we consider, that there are many benevolent affections planted in our constitution, whose exertions make a capital part of our good and enjoyment; from these considerations, this principle leads us also, though more indirectly, to the practice of justice, humanity, and all the social virtues. (AP, 163–164)

Reid's notion that the line from the idea of our good on the whole to "the practice of justice, humanity, and all the social virtues" is somewhat indirect indicates that, although rational concern for our good on the whole and the rationality embedded in morality commend the same courses of action, their principles are actually quite different:

> A sense of interest may induce us to do this, when a suitable reward is set before us. But there is a nobler principle in the constitution of man, which, in many cases, gives a clearer and more certain rule of conduct, than a regard merely to interest would give, and a principle, without which man would not be a moral agent.
>
> A man is prudent when he consults his real interest, but he cannot be virtuous, if he has no regard to duty. (AP, 169)

The second avenue Reid's botanical metaphors invite us to explore is moral development. Seeds grow and take on new properties in the process. However, they do not do this without assistance. This makes evident the need for care and nurtures from *others* if the child is to develop morally or otherwise. Thus, Reid says:

> The power of vegetation in the seed of a plant, without heat and moisture, would for ever lie dormant. The rational and moral powers of man would perhaps lie dormant without instruction and example. Yet these powers are a part, and the noblest part, of his constitution; as the power of vegetation is of the seed. (AP, 279)

If we are concerned with how we might best nurture the child's "seeds of morality," attending carefully to the developmental features of childhood is necessary. This, Reid would say, is a matter of some *practical*, moral importance. This is so from two vantage points. First, adults have special responsibilities to aid this development. But, second, as children develop, they acquire moral standing and responsibilities in their own right—as children, not simply as potential adults. This, too, should be respected. But, if we reflect on childhood and moral development in these ways, might we learn some things that will help us, as adults, answer our own questions about morality?

Reid's answer would likely be, yes. After all, we were once children. We *grew* into adulthood *from* childhood. We may not remember well (or at all) our earlier years, but it does not follow, of course, that these formative years have had no lasting effect on who we are now—and even how we *should* be now.

Reid says that the child's earliest grasp of moral relations is most likely through observing the behavior of others:

> Our first moral conceptions are probably got by attending coolly to the conduct of others, and observing what moves our approbation, what our indignation. These sentiments spring from our moral faculty as naturally as the sensations of sweet and bitter from the faculty of taste. They have their natural objects. (AP, 279)

It should be noted that, although this observing is done "cooly," this does not imply an absence of affect. *Sentiments*, a blending of affect and judgment, arise "naturally," says Reid. By comparing this with the sensations of sweet and bitter, he is emphasizing that these first moral conceptions are not dependent on a process of *reasoning* (inference from premises to conclusion). However, as moral conceptions they imply *reason*, in that having a *conception* involves understanding, or the grasp of ideas, including some understanding of both differences and similarity among ideas. Only those with rational capacities (reason) can have such moral conceptions.

Examples of both appropriate and inappropriate conduct typically surround children. This can pose a serious problem because, with Aristotle, Reid says that the human being "is an imitative animal." This is a partly instinctive "proneness to imitation." Although we are disposed to imitate what we naturally approve, in some areas we learn more by example than rule. In fact, says Reid, "human nature disposes us to the imitation of those among whom we live, when we neither desire nor will it" (AP, 84). This is evident in picking up dialects, especially in the case of the very young.

Given that the natural disposition to imitate may not be restricted to morally appropriate conduct, there is a need to make sure that children are provided with examples of moral conduct along with evident approval by others. Meanwhile, children form many beliefs before their rational faculties have matured:

> [...] [B]efore we grow up to the full use of our rational faculties, we do believe, and must believe, many things without any evidence at all [...]. The faculties which we have in common with brute animals are of earlier growth than reason. We are irrational animals for a considerable time before we can properly be called rational. (AP, 85)

One propensity very young children share with the "brutes" is what Joseph Butler calls "sudden resentment"—a defensive, communicative response to apparent threats and to being hurt. What Butler, Reid, and Adam Smith (in his *Theory of Moral Sentiments*) all discuss is how this "sudden resentment" needs to be displaced either by resentment that can be well-grounded (a form of "deliberate resentment") or by something other than resentment in any of its forms (when, as is often the case, there is nothing that one can reasonably resent—that is, no proper object). We might call this the need for *taming* resentment.[10]

However, this taming requires the use of reason if it is to yield a sentiment that can fairly be called *reasonable*. This takes us directly into the social environment within which children develop their rational and moral powers. Acquiring the use of reason at all, says Reid, would never happen if we "were not brought into the society of reasonable creatures" (AP, 86). Empirical support for this, he suggests, can be found in historical accounts of "wild men" brought up from early childhood outside of human society. Although we know of few examples of such individuals and, therefore, cannot be entirely confident of what to say about them, Reid says:

> But all I have heard of agreed in this, that the wild man gave but very slender indications of the rational faculties; and with regard to his mind, was hardly distinguishable from the more sagacious of the brutes. (AP, 85)

How does being reared in a "society of reasonable creatures" help us develop our rational capacities? Reid says:

> The benefit he [the child] receives from society is derived partly from imitation of what he sees others do, partly from the instruction and information they communicate to him, without which he could be neither preserved from destruction, nor acquire the use of his rational powers. (AP, 86)

So, the child's long-term well-being is at stake in the acquisition of rational powers. However, this result should not be confused with whatever motivation, intentions, or purposes that might be involved in acquiring these powers. The same is true of moral powers (which, as already indicated, require at least some rational powers). Reid's reliance on the "seeds of moral discernment"

---

10 See my "Taming Resentment," in *New Essays on Adam Smith's Moral Philosophy*, Wade L. Robison and David B. Suits, eds. (Rochester, NY: RIT Press, 2012), pp. 151–172.

makes little, if any, reference to motives, intentions, or purposes that a child might have for acquiring either rational or moral powers. But he does discuss some crucial factors that are involved in their development.

As they move from infancy into early childhood, says Reid, children have "everything to learn." He continues:

> [I]n order to learn, they must believe their instructors: they need a greater stock of faith from infancy to twelve or fourteen than ever after [...]. They believe a thousand things before they ever spend a thought upon evidence. Nature supplies the want of evidence, and gives the man instinctive kind of faith without evidence [...]. They believe implicitly whatever they are told, and receive with assurance the testimony of every one, without ever thinking of a reason why they should do so. (AP, 86–87)

But, one might ask, how is this possible? Reid's answer is that, prior to acquiring an explicit grasp of basic moral ideas, the child's behavior can be seen to conform to certain principles. There are two in particular that Reid emphasizes. The first is a *principle of credulity*, whereby the child believes, without a critical appraisal, whatever he/she is told by others. The second is a *principle of veracity*, whereby the child says whatever he/she takes to be true. Although both principles require some degree of rational ability and trust, neither is yet a moral principle. Later the child will learn that sometimes distrust in the word of others is warranted, if not wise; and the child will learn how to lie (and why this may be an attractive option on occasion).

That there are these two principles is, for Reid, an empirically supportable claim. That the "hard knocks" of experience lead children to modify their trust in the word of others, as well as their disposition to say what they think, is also an empirically supportable claim. However, this still leaves the question of what role the principles of credulity and veracity and their modifications might play in the *moral* development of the child.

Not surprisingly, as children experience "hard knocks" in their uncritical reliance on the principles of credulity and veracity, they experience frustration and anger—both theirs (when let down by others) and others' (when they let down others). These confrontational moments are normatively loaded (e.g., approval/disapproval, should/ought). The social environment is one in which it at some point it becomes clear to the child that, even in moments of "cool" appraisal (of oneself or others), there is *normative* concern, not simply concern to "get the facts straight."

Still, there is a natural, human desire to "get the facts straight." As Reid puts it:

> [...] the desire of knowledge in the human species, is a principle that cannot escape our observation.
>
> The curiosity of children is the principle that occupies most of their time while they are awake. What they can handle they examine on all sides, and often break in pieces, in order to discover what is within. (AP, 100)

Furthermore, "the desire of knowledge is not more natural than is the desire of communicating our knowledge" (AP, 105). This desire of communicating our knowledge, Reid says, is connected with our desire for esteem, which "can have no possible gratification but in society" (AP, 105).

So, children meaningfully enter into the *social* world at a very early age. However, Reid says, they are voluntary agents in that world long before they make significant use of their rational capacities. Reason and the virtues "come to maturity by slow degrees, and are too weak, in the greater part of the species, to secure the preservation of individuals and of communities, and to produce that varied scene of human life, in which they are to be exercised and improved" (AP, 106).

Just as children do not *reason* their way into the social world of rationality, at some point (Reid cannot say exactly when) they become capable of two basic kinds of "operations of the mind": the *solitary* and the *social* (AP, 330). Solitary operations of the mind "may be performed by a man in solitude, without intercourse with any other intelligent being." "A man may see, and hear, and remember, and judge, and reason; he may deliberate and form purposes, and execute them, without the intervention of any other intelligent being. They are solitary acts." (Note, however, that this does mean that those capable of these solitary acts could have done so without having at some time been in social contact with other intelligent beings—as Reid's discussion of the "wild boy" suggests. Such social contact, he might say, is necessary for the child to develop the ability to perform certain kinds of solitary operations of the mind.)

However, says Reid, social operations of the mind "necessarily imply social intercourse with some other intelligent being who bears a part in them" (AP, 330). They indicate a power "of holding social intercourse with [one's] kind, by asking and refusing, threatening and supplicating, commanding and obeying, testifying and promising, [...]" (AP, 331) These social operations, Reid says, "appear to be as simple in their nature as the solitary. They are found in every individual of the species, even before the use of reason" (AP, 331).[11]

It is from this ability to perform social operations of the mind (and receptivity to the social operations of the minds of others) that the child can eventually (actually, very soon) understand social operations of the mind as having moral significance. So, this original ability (which is not the result of reasoning from other premises but is still dependent on reason for its eventual contribution to the child's moral development) is part of what Reid has in mind when he refers to "the seeds of morality."

Moral ideas seem somehow to "grow from," without necessarily being "reasoned from," earlier forms of trust, anger, empathy, and reciprocity. Imitation seems to play as strong a role in their development as reasoning. At some point, Reid says, we find ourselves with first principles that seem to us to be self-evident. A powerful reason for not wanting to let go of them, and for wanting them to develop in our children, is that the very viability of a tolerable, not to speak of a flourishing, social life depends on their being taken seriously. However, it does not follow that this is recognized by children as they come to acquire them, or that these first principles themselves focus directly on their "private" or "public utility." For example, the primary reason one should not punish the innocent is that they are *innocent*. That observing this principle supports private and public utility is good. But, for Reid, that the innocent should not be punished is a principle of justice whose primary focus is on the innocent themselves rather than public utility . Similarly, one should keep one's promises because of what it is to promise, not simply because this may also have public utility.[12]

Reid offers his account of the moral development of children, not as a "proof" that moral judgments are "true" (something to which he is otherwise committed), but as an account of how morality enters into our lives and as a reminder of its importance to us—and even of its fragility, dependent as it is on properly nurturing the "seeds of morality." Is it possible that our "moral sense" is unreliable, no matter how carefully we attend to it—or that it may simply be in some sense "illusory"? Yes, Reid might say, but in just

---

11 Before the use of reason, says Reid. However, bearing in mind the distinction between reason and reasoning (inference-making), it seems that Reid must here be referring to the latter. Insofar as promising, and other forms of social communication require conceptual understanding, reason is involved.

12 The case of promising will be explored below in detail in Chapter 5, "The Premise of a Promise."

the same way that this is possible for all of our senses. All of these senses (including our moral sense), he says, come from the "same mint." All of our mature senses involve *judgment* in their employment. All are corrigible. But all, as far as we can tell, are to some extent capable of self-correction. So, Reid concludes, the skeptic cannot be "refuted," but no good reason has been given for doubting the general reliability of our senses, including our moral sense if our gardens are tended well.

Chapter 3

SMITH'S "IMPARTIAL SPECTATOR"[1]

Adam Smith's account of moral development draws heavily from Joseph Butler's earlier account of resentment and forgiveness in his Sermon VIII, "Upon Resentment," and Sermon IX, "Upon the Forgiveness of Injuries" (*Fifteen Sermons*).[2] Smith opens his *Theory of the Moral Sentiments* with the assertion that human selfishness is limited, as evidenced by our getting some pleasure from seeing the happiness of others.[3] Further, even "the greatest ruffian, the most hardened violator of the laws of society" is susceptible to having some degree of pity or compassion for the misery of others. So, he concludes, some of our sympathies express genuine concern about others, not just ourselves.

Readers might expect Smith next to say more about our positive concern about the happiness of others. Instead, he turns to what he calls our "unsocial passions"—most notably, *resentment*. Unpleasant in itself, nevertheless resentment seeks a sympathetic audience. However, until we can see why someone is resentful, our reaction to the display of this passion is itself quite negative. In fact, resentment should be viewed as suspect, at least initially. Smith alerts us:

> There is no passion, of which the human mind is capable, concerning whose justice we ought to be so doubtful, concerning whose indulgence we ought so carefully to consult our natural sense of propriety, or so diligently to consider what will be the sentiments of the cool and impartial spectator.

1 Much of this chapter is based on portions of my "Taming Resentment," published in *New Essays on Adam Smith's Moral Philosophy*, David Suits and Wade L. Robison (eds.) (Rochester, NY: RIT Press, 2012), 151–165.

2 In Joseph Butler, *Fifteen Sermons*, edited by T.A. Roberts (London: Society for Promoting Christian Knowledge, 1970).

3 Adam Smith, *The Theory of Moral Sentiments*, D.D. Raphael and A.L. Macfie (eds.) (Indianapolis: Liberty Fund, Inc., 1984.) The original 6th edition was published in 1790. Page references will be to TMS in the main text of this chapter.

In fact, insofar as it is merely an expression of hatred and anger, he adds, resentment is "the greatest poison to the happiness of a good mind" (TMS, 37).

Nevertheless, says Smith, suitably restrained, resentment can function as "the safeguard of justice and the security of innocence" (TMS, 79). It can be a defensive response that "prompts us to beat off the mischief which is attempted to be done to us, and to retaliate that which is already done; that the offender may be made to repent of his injustice, and that others through fear of the like punishment, may be terrified from being guilty of the like offense" (TMS, 79).

This, Smith believes, is how resentment *ought* to function when at its moral best. However, in fact, it is prone to various excesses; and it is one of the tasks of moral education to help us to learn to resist these excesses. This normally begins in childhood. Smith says:

> A very young child has no self-command; but, whatever are its emotions, whether fear, or grief, or anger, it endeavours always, by the violence of its outcries, to alarm, as much as it can, the attention of its nurse, or of its parents. While it remains under the custody of such partial protectors, its anger is the first and, perhaps, the only passion which it is taught to moderate. (TMS, 145)

Although young children may learn to moderate their anger to some extent in their home settings, venturing away from home can present them with a rude shock. A child's dominating self-absorption is unlikely to be well received among peers outside the family:

> [The child] naturally wishes to gain their favour, and to avoid their hatred or contempt. Regard even to its own safety teaches it to do so; and it soon finds that it can do so in no other way than by moderating, not only its anger, but all its other passions, to the degree which its play-fellows and companions are likely to be pleased with. It thus enters into the great school of self-command, it studies to be more and more master of itself, and begins to exercise over its own feelings a discipline which the practice of the longest life is very seldom sufficient to bring to complete perfection. (TMS, 145)

However, Smith says, we do need the company of others. Without their feedback, self-assessment is not possible. In such circumstances one "is provided with no mirror which can present [one's character] to his view. Bring him into society, and he is immediately provided with the mirror which he wanted before" (TMS, 110).

This "mirror" serves as our first critic. Judged by others, we become concerned with how we seem to them:

> We begin, upon this account, to examine our own passions and conduct, and to consider how these must appear to them, by considering how they would appear to us if in their situation. We suppose ourselves the spectators of our own behaviour, and endeavour to imagine what effect it would, in this light, produce upon us. This is the only looking-glass by which we can, in some measure, with the eyes of other people, scrutinize the propriety of our own conduct. (TMS, 112)

Although we want the approval of others, Smith says that this is not enough to make us fit for society. We also need, normatively, to desire "what ought to be approved of" (TMS, 114). But this second desire can be satisfied only by becoming "impartial spectators of our own character and conduct" (TMS, 114). Smith concludes, "This self-approbation, if not the only, is at least the principal object, about which he can or ought to be anxious. The love of it, is the love of virtue" (TMS, 117). This desire for "what ought to be approved of" calls for *judgment*, and therefore reason in the form of a cognitive ability to conceptualize which candidates are available for possible approval and to make some assessment of their respective *worthiness* of approval.

Zeroing in on how resentment fares in all of this, Smith points out the difficulties the person who expresses resentment has in winning the sympathy of those who initially witness it. Resentment is not a happy state of mind. Given this, says Smith, we are more anxious for our friends to "enter into our resentments" than for them to "enter into our gratitude."

However, resentment is among those "unsocial passions" that initially "serve rather to disgust and provoke us against them" (TMS, 11). That is, until others understand the basis for the resentment one is expressing, it is more likely that they will empathize with the targets of that resentment. So, the bearer of resentment needs to learn how to overcome the inclination of others to side with the target of resentment rather than its bearer. But this can be a heavy burden to bear.

In dealing successfully with this challenge, the resenter needs to realize that the "compassion of the spectator must arise altogether from the consideration of what he himself would feel if he was reduced to the same unhappy situation, and, what perhaps is impossible, was at the same time able to regard it with his present reason and judgment" (TMS, 12). The resenter must try first to see things as the spectator does, who initially is likely to side with those who are the object of aggression. So, for resentment to be seen as "graceful and agreeable, it must be more humbled and brought down below that pitch to which it would naturally rise, than almost any other passion" (TMS, 34).

One function of this humbling of resentment is to place a needed check on the natural preference we have for ourselves. Smith observes:

> Though it may be true, therefore, that every individual, in his own breast, naturally prefers himself to all mankind, yet he dares not look mankind in the face, and avow that he acts according to this principle. He feels that in this preference they can never go along with him, and that how natural soever it may be to him, it must always appear excessive and extravagant to them. (TMS, 83)

Shifting in this way to a third-person perspective has a leveling effect, moving one in the direction of impartiality:

> When he views himself in the light in which he is conscious that others will view him, he sees that to them he is but one of the multitude in no respect better than any other in it. If he would act so that the impartial spectator may enter into the principles of his conduct, which is what of all things he has the greatest desire to do, he must, upon this, as upon all other occasions, humble the arrogance of his self-love, and bring it down to something which other men can go along with. (TMS, 83)

It is only by staying within these constraints that one can realistically hope to have one's resentment endorsed by others. This is a social process, especially when one's resentment is clearly excessive. For Smith, the *dignity* of a passion is a reflection of the "recollection and self-command" it expresses. Untamed, resentment is excessive and undignified. The *propriety* of resentment requires a "certain mediocrity" (TMS, 27). When it matches this, it expresses the *indignation* of an impartial spectator, "which allows no word, no gesture, to escape it beyond what this more equitable sentiment would dictate; which never, even in thought, attempts any greater vengeance, nor desires to inflict any greater punishment, than what every indifferent person would rejoice to see executed" (TMS, 24). It is only when resentment takes on the form of indignation of this sort that it can be said to be properly contained. We are not disposed to sympathize with those exhibiting resentment "before we are informed of the cause which excites them." (TMS, 36) Thus, Smith insists, there are several conditions that must be met before spectators will *thoroughly* sympathize with our resentment (TMS, 38):

- The cause must be severe enough that others would regard it as contemptible if one didn't "in some measure" resent it.

- Resentment should be tempered by the seriousness of the offense.
- Our resentment is best experienced as if by another, more from a sense of the propriety of resentment than from a more directly felt passion.
- Our resentment must be borne with dignity (magnanimity). Expressions of it must be "plain, open, and direct; determined without positiveness, and elevated without insolence; not only free from petulance and low scurrility, but generous, candid, and full of proper regards, even for the person who has offended us."
- The passion must not appear to have "extinguished our humanity." Revenge must be taken "with reluctance, from necessity, and in consequence of great and repeated provocations."

He concludes: "When resentment is guarded and qualified in this manner, it may be admitted to be even generous and noble" (TMS, 38).

Smith holds that our sense of justice is not derived from a direct concern for public utility. In contrast, his friend David Hume claims that the sentiment of justice is derived either from our reflecting on the tendency of justice to promote public utility or from some "simple original instinct, and is not ascertained by any argument or reflection."[4]

Hume includes resentment in his list of "simple original instincts." However, rather than picking up on Butler's account of the role of reflection in transforming "sudden resentment" into "deliberate resentment," Hume focuses on property and public utility. Smith agrees that justice does serve public utility. However, he says:

[I]t is not the view of this utility or hurtfulness which is either the first or principal source of our approbation and disapprobation [...]. [I]t will be found, upon examination, that the usefulness of any disposition of mind is seldom the first ground of our approbation; and that the sentiment of approbation always involves in it a sense of propriety quite distinct from the perception of utility. (TMS, 188–189)

Furthermore, when it is an expression of our sense of justice, resentment is "a passion which is never properly called forth but by actions which tend to do real and positive hurt to some particular persons" (TMS, 79).

---

4 David Hume, *An Enquiry Concerning the Principles of Morals*, Tom L. Beauchamp (ed.) (Oxford, 1998), 96.

Regarding either the destruction or loss of a single man, or the loss of a single guinea that is part of a thousand guineas, Smith insists:

> In neither case does our regard for the individuals arise from our regard for the multitude: but in both cases our regard for the multitude is compounded and made up of the particular regards which we feel for the different individuals of which it is composed. As when a small sum is unjustly taken from us, we do not so much prosecute the injury from a regard to the preservation of our whole fortune, as from a regard to that particular sum which we have lost; so when a single man is injured, or destroyed, we demand the punishment of the wrong that has been done to him, not so much from a concern for the general interest of society, as from a concern for that very individual who has been injured [...]. (TMS, 89–90)

Smith consistently distinguishes the *resulting* public utility of justice from our *motives* for justice. Also, even as he points out the usefulness of moral rules, he introduces them as a way of combating self-serving self-deception rather than as a means to public utility. A major worry for Smith is our susceptibility to self-deception, which he sees as a "fatal weakness of mankind, {and] the source of half the disorders of human life" (TMS, 158).

The most effective remedy, Smith suggests, is the observance of "certain general rules concerning what is fit and proper either to be done or to be avoided" (TMS, 159). These rules express in general form what in particular instances we, when clear-headed, approve or disapprove. But it is important to realize that our original approval or disapproval of actions falling under these rules is not that a particular action falls under a general rule:

> The general rule, on the contrary, is formed, by finding from experience, that all actions of a certain kind, or circumstanced in a certain manner, are approved or disapproved of [...]. [One's] detestation of this crime, it is evident, would arise instantaneously and antecedent to his having formed to himself any such general rule. The general rule, on the contrary, which he might afterwards form, would be founded upon the detestation which he felt necessarily arise in his own breast, at the thought of this, and every other particular action of the same kind. (TMS, 159–160)

If we acquire a habit of respecting these general rules, we can avoid doing what is contrary to what we would otherwise directly see as objectionable if we were not blinded by excessive partiality to ourselves. As for the relationship between general rules and public utility, Smith comments:

> The administration of the great system of the universe, however, the care of the universal happiness of all rational and sensible beings, is the business of god and not of man. To man is allotted a much humbler department, but one much more suitable to the weakness of his powers, and to the narrowness of his comprehension; the care of his own happiness, of that of his family, his friends, his country. (TMS, 237)

However, as ideal as Smith's notion of an impartial spectator might seem like a standard for correcting resentment's excesses, he admits that the standard it sets is not fully achievable. However, some argue that matters are much worse than Smith imagines.[5] Virgil Henry Storr and Henrietta John maintain that what Smith's impartial spectator could provide, at best, is a social "mirror" that expresses our own enculturization, rather than disinterested assessment. Thus, the socialized individual may end up being a "quite parochial figure" (Storr and John, 33). What assurance is there that the cultural values surrounding the developing child will be free from the sort of bias that seriously compromises the hoped for disinterested perspective of an impartial spectator? Smith himself expresses concern that the vast majority of adults fall well short of attaining an impartial perspective, even with the aid of others as social "mirrors." Ignorance, unruly passions, biased convention, and widespread "self-deceit" are the primary culprits.

Matters become even more challenging when we consider different cultures. Here Storr and John employ the metaphor of "cultural spectacles." They contend that our moral perspectives are formed by social processes that challenge any ambition to embrace substantive, universal features of morality. Instead, it is more plausible to see us as looking at the world through "cultural spectacles," thereby raising the specter of moral relativism. Storr and John's suggested way of dealing with the problems this poses is to

---

5 Storr, Virgil and Henrietta John, "The Impersonal Spectator's Cultural Spectacles," in *Of Sympathy and Selfishness*, C.S. Thomas, (ed.) (Mercer University Press, 2015). The commentary on Storr and John that follows is coauthored with Elaine E. Englehardt as a part of "18th Century Scottish Philosophers and Children," presented at the 2017 International Council for Philosophical Inquiry With Children (ICPIC) program in Madrid, Spain.

encourage more dialogue across different cultures. However, they note that the very notion of an impartial spectator "evolves through a process of enculturation, and, as such, the imagined impartial spectator is, like all of us, a cultural creature" (Storr and John, 51). They worry that, even at its best, the perspective of an impartial spectator will be affected to some extent by the particularities of the culture within which that perspective has developed. Thus, they worry about any claims to "universality" that one might make from that perspective.

Nevertheless, Storr and John conclude somewhat optimistically: "On a more positive note, however, we should expect that the more we encounter people different from ourselves, the more our passions are moderated, and more cultured our spectator becomes. Thus, the more cosmopolitan our lives, the more understanding, tolerant, and cosmopolitan our views become" (Storr and John, 51–52).

Why we might expect such results is not explained. However, Storr and John provide the germs of an answer that Smith might find suggestive. Here is how they describe the process of enculturation: "Wanting to receive praise and to avoid blame, we simply try to act as others around us act. However, since other people can be biased, we realize that other people's feelings toward us are not always the best barometer of our actions. Thus, the impartial spectator within us becomes our judge as we seek to become people who are 'objectively' worthy of praise and innocent of blame. To judge us at all, the impartial spectator needs a lens to help it discern the right and wrong in our actions, and that lens is our culture" (Storr and John, 51).

Although Storr and John insist that "the spectator's judgments are culturally specific," it seems that room is provided for at least some of the spectator's judgments to be critical of the judgments of others, and even one's own. This is acknowledged by Storr and John's statement that "we realize that other people's feelings toward us are not always the best barometer of our actions." So, it is possible for a culture to encourage self-criticism rather than simply social convention. Smith himself found fault with much of the world that immediately surrounded him, as well as such practices as slavery in far-away lands.

Did Smith believe that children were capable of entering into a philosophical discussion with other children, and even with adults, about what is better, what is worse, fair, unfair, kind, cruel, insufficient, excessive, and so on? It is interesting, and important, to note that the students who heard his lectures at Glasgow were typically young teenagers (as were Reid's). One would certainly hope that he believed they were capable of understanding, and putting into practice, the critical perspective he was advocating.

Nevertheless, those who today advocate establishing communities of inquiry in the schools need to take Storr and John's challenge of "cultural spectacles" seriously. A note of optimism, however, is that if these communities of inquiry are started early enough, the "enculturization" that concerns Storr and John will not yet have fully set in. Combined with the inclusion of the serious study of other cultures in early education, establishing philosophical communities of inquiry in the schools would seem to hold some promise in addressing their concerns.

Chapter 4

REASON AND SENTIMENT
IN MORALITY

Much has been made of the notion that there are foundational differences between David Hume and Thomas Reid's accounts of morality, with Hume allegedly emphasizing moral sentiments and Reid emphasizing the role of reason. However, despite Hume's early relegation of reason to the role of being merely a servant of the passions in his *Treatise* (T), later in the opening paragraphs of his *Enquiry Concerning the Principles of Morals* (EPM) he makes a strident attack on moral skeptics who, he says, shun common sense and reason.

Adam Smith offers a third account, one that aligns well in part with both Hume and Reid. This chapter will discuss these accounts in relation to one another. Its conclusion is that, although significant differences among the three can, indeed, be found, all of them contend their views are grounded in empirically observable features of our human constitution, including both reason and sentiment.

However, observable these features may be, accounts of their contributions to morality require carefully attending to how they develop in childhood. Fortunately, Reid's *Essays on the Active Powers of Man* (AP) and Smith's *Theory of the Moral Sentiments* (TMS) attempt this. Unfortunately, Hume's writings do not. Still, all three philosophers give us reason to conclude that children, not just adults, are capable of significant critical thinking about moral issues, and that it is important that this be encouraged.

Hume's *Treatise* (T) and *Enquiry Concerning the Principles of Morality* (EPM) contend that morality is grounded in sentiment, with reason playing an important, but secondary, role in moral life. Reason's basic moral contribution is to reveal facts that can show us ways of achieving certain desirable ends and avoiding certain undesirable actions. However, the ends themselves come to life through sentiments of approval or disapproval which can move us to act in one way or another. Reason alone does not determine these ends. In the final analysis, it is sentiment, not reason, that grounds moral values and action. Without moral sentiments among humans, there is no moral work for reason to do.

For Reid, too, moral sentiments are essential for morality. However, in seeming contrast to Hume, these sentiments include reason within their structure, as their make-up includes moral judgments, which involve conceptualizations that only rational creatures can have. This does not mean that reason alone determines moral judgment. Reid's *Active Powers* discusses at great length how reason and sentiments work together to shape the moral judgments expressed in our decisions and actions.

Smith's *Theory of Moral Sentiments* also offers a detailed account of how sentiments in children become moral. At their best, moral agents strive to base their judgments on what they believe would be approved by an imagined impartial spectator who regards each moral agent as only one among many. Young children can have some grasp of the idea of impartiality, but as Smith and his critics agree, even adults commonly fail to satisfy this standard. In any case, as Smith shows, reason has an essential role to play in striving to grasp what a more impartial perspective requires.

Hume's *Enquiry* sets the stage for much of what Reid has to say. Near its end, in Appendix I, "Concerning Moral Sentiment," Hume finally fulfills his earlier promise of explicitly addressing the question of the relation of sentiment and reason in morality. He discusses features of our natural constitution that he believes have a bearing on the foundations of morality. Most basic is a general *principle of humanity*, supported by common sentiments such as benevolence and gratitude that we can expect to find anywhere there are gatherings of humans. We are first and foremost *social* creatures.

Hume's *Enquiry* says surprisingly little about the conditions that aid the development and refinement of moral sentiments. But he does believe they reveal the defining features of morality—all of which he thinks ultimately serve public utility. It is this that provides support for and helps clarify the value of justice, which centers around notions of property that depend on the conventional rules of particular political states.

Hume offers his empirically supportable account in opposition to views that depend on *a priori* rationalistic assumptions. Despite being commonly thought to rely on such assumptions, Reid also bases his account on what he takes to be empirical observations. Like Hume, Reid cites features of our natural constitution that seem empirically evident to him. So, articulating the differences between their accounts requires examining nuances of their empirical claims.

At the outset of his *Enquiry Concerning the Principles of Morals* (EPM, 73) Hume indicates that he has no patience with those who deny the *reality* of moral distinctions. Those, he says, who are "pertinaciously obstinate in their principles," or who are "entirely disingenuous, who really do not believe the opinions they defend," are beyond disputing, and cannot be engaged in serious argumentation. However, left to themselves, says Hume, they finally will, "from mere weariness, come over to the side of *common sense and reason*" (Emph. added).

However, near the end of EPM, confident that, even from the standpoint of self-interest, he had successfully shown the superiority of virtue over vice in nearly every instance, Hume considers one last doubt. In the case of justice, he asks what we should say about a *sensible knave*, who appreciates the advantages rules of justice provide, but thinks that further gains may be possible by making himself an exception to the rules. Such a knave, while acknowledging the importance of justice for society (and himself), "may think that an act of iniquity or infidelity will make a considerable addition to his fortune, without causing any considerable breach in the social union and confederacy" (EPM, 155).

For such acts of iniquity or infidelity to be successful, deception is required to maintain the appearance of being fully supportive of justice. So, it seems we have two features of such acts that contribute to their wrongfulness. First, they are acts of *iniquity*, thereby wronging others. Second, they are acts of *dishonesty*, thereby deliberately attempting to deceive others. In regard to dishonesty, Hume represents the sensible knave as thinking:

> That *honesty is the best policy*, may be a good general rule, but is liable to many exceptions; and he, it may perhaps be thought, conducts himself with most wisdom, who observes the general rule, and takes advantage of all the exceptions. (EPM, 155)

Might such a thought also occur to others—those who do not regard themselves to be sensible knaves? Yes, says Hume; but it should not take much for such a person to reject the sensible knave's "wisdom," especially if the heart is allowed to rule:

> If his heart rebel not against such pernicious maxims, baseness, he has indeed lost a considerable motive to virtue [...]. But in all ingenuous natures, the antipathy to treachery and roguery is too strong to be counter-balanced by any views of profit or pecuniary advantage. Inward peace of mind, consciousness of integrity, a satisfactory review of our own conduct; these are circumstances very requisite to happiness, and will be cherished and cultivated by every honest man, who feels the importance of them. (EPM, 155)

Knaves, Hume adds, seem willing to trade their integrity, and even their happiness, for "worthless toys and gewgaws" (EPM, 156).

Adam Smith likely agreed with this. However, he might not have realized that Joseph Butler's earlier account of resentment actually challenges certain features of Hume's response to the sensible knave. Thomas Reid did. While agreeing with the sentiments Hume attributes to "honest men," Reid wondered how Hume could effectively employ them, given his view of justice and the importance each of us apparently attaches to self-interest. The sensible knave, after all, seems to attend to both justice and self-interest. If convinced that making himself an exception to the rules of justice will harm the public interest, he will refrain. In fact, like others, *publicly* he supports the rules; such a public stance is essential for the system to work. But this does not necessarily require one *privately* to agree. Of course, publicly denouncing what one privately approves for oneself is a form of duplicity. Still, by hypothesis, in this case, it is not contrary to the public interest—and it does serve one's self-interest. So, what is *wrong* with it?

The unhappiness Hume attributes to those who might actually settle for "worthless toys and gewgaws" is presumably the result of a stricken conscience; such individuals, he says, cannot sustain "consciousness of integrity, a satisfactory review of [their] own conduct." Smith and Reid would undoubtedly agree. Morally, for Hume, what else is there to be concerned about? Reid attempts to supply something else, but at a cost to Hume. Hume must either accept what Reid offers and thereby concede that our sentiment of justice is not derived solely from public utility, or he must admit that he has no fully adequate response to the sensible knave's challenge.

While Hume confines his notion of justice to property in relation to public utility, Reid identifies six "branches" of justice. Reid classifies four of them as *natural*, as distinct from *acquired*, rights: "the right of an innocent man to the safety of his person and family, to his liberty and reputation" (AP, 313). The fifth concerns the making and keeping of promises, while only the sixth concerns property. Reid does not claim that his list is complete. But he does contend that it represents commonly held moral convictions.

It is likely that Smith would agree with much of what Reid says here. In fact, Smith explicitly remarks:

> There is no greater tormentor of the human breast than violent resentment which cannot be gratified. An innocent man, brought to the scaffold by the false imputation of an infamous or odious crime, suffers the most cruel misfortune which it is possible for innocence to suffer [...]. The innocent man, on the contrary, over and above the uneasiness which this fear may occasion, is tormented by his own indignation at the injustice which has been done to him. (TMS, 119–120)]

Although Reid casts much of his account of justice in terms of rights, equally important is his account of the role of resentment. Reid says that when we sense that our rights are violated, we feel *injured*. But *injury* and *hurt* are distinct. Humans and animals alike naturally respond to *hurt* with what Butler calls "sudden resentment"—a defensive mechanism that expresses anger toward the purported cause of the hurt. As Reid puts it:

> Every action that gives pain or uneasiness produces resentment. This is common to man before the use of reason, and to the more sagacious brutes; and it shews no conception of justice in either. (AP, 309)

However, as human reason develops, the notion that resentment needs a "proper and formal object" also develops. This is Butler's "deliberate resentment," which includes a rational element. Reid continues:

> If we consider, on the other hand, what an injury is which is the object of the natural passion of resentment, every man, capable of reflection, perceives that an injury implies more than being hurt. If I be hurt by a stone falling out of the wall, or by a flash of lightning, or by a convulsive and involuntary motion of another man's arm, no injury is done, no resentment raised in a man who has reason. In this, as in all moral actions, there must be the will and intention of the agent to do the hurt. (AP, 310)

It is important for Reid's account of resentment that, although "deliberate resentment" is not present at birth, its emergence is "natural" in the sense that "these sentiments spring up in the mind of man as naturally as his body grows to its proper stature" (AP, 313–314). Although the particular forms these sentiments take on may vary somewhat with the instruction provided by "parents, priests, philosophers, or politicians," the seeds for their development are present prior to any instruction (AP, 314).

Reid does not mean that our sense of justice develops prior to socialization with others. He concedes to Hume:

> that men have no conception of the virtue of justice til they have lived some time in society. It is purely a moral conception, and our moral conceptions and moral judgments are not born with us. They grow up by degrees, as our reason does. (AP, 305–306)

Furthermore, Reid acknowledges that he does not know exactly when, or in what order, our moral conceptions develop. However, like Smith, what he does claim is that the idea of public utility arises only *after* we already have a rather well-developed sense of justice. So, from a *developmental* point of view, our concept of justice is not derived solely from that of public utility. Reid insists that:

> every man is conscious of a specific difference between the resentment he feels for an injury done to himself, and his indignation against a wrong done to the public. (AP, 314)

It is this distinction that is crucial to Reid's reply to the sensible knave, but which seems to be slighted in Hume's account. A judge, Reid says, can be expected to consider the public good when punishing someone for a private injury, but this "seldom enters into the thought of the injured person" (AP, 314). This, Reid adds, is reflected in the criminal law, which distinguishes the redress due to the victim from redress due to the public. Hume might reply, however, that justice does not come into play until the public good is considered. Smith and Reid disagree, as their accounts of resentment make clear.

While Hume attempts to derive justice from utility, Reid claims the idea of justice is inseparable from the notions of *favor* and *injury* (as distinct from *hurt*):

> [A] favour, an act of justice, and an injury, are so related to one another, that he who conceives one must conceive the other two. They lie, as it were, in one line, and resemble the relations of greater, less, and equal [...] . In a like manner, of those actions by which we profit or hurt other men, a favour is more than justice, an injury is less; and that which is neither a favour nor an injury is a just action. (AP, 311)

Favor is linked with gratitude, injury with resentment. Insofar as gratitude and resentment involve understanding and judgment, they embrace the conceptions of justice and injustice.

However, moral sentiments for Hume must meet a test of *generality*, which for him seems to invoke a notion of public utility. Natural gratitude, resentment, and even benevolence are premoral, directed as they are at only this or that particular object. Only *enlarged* sentiments are inclusive enough to count as moral. But Hume conceives of the moral enlargement of sentiments in only one way—that of public utility, as expressed in his principle of humanity. This seems to imply that sentiment is moral only if it is somehow directed toward the good of the larger public. This is the force of his notion that the sentiment of justice is derived solely from public utility.

Reid thinks of the enlargement of sentiments differently. The transition from "sudden resentment" to "deliberate resentment," introduces undeniably *rational* features. As Reid puts it, "The feeling of his heart arises from the judgment of his understanding" (AP, 313). If I am the sufferer of wrongdoing, I will feel resentment on my own behalf. However, it must be added that Reid accepts a notion of universalizability (the "law of the prophets") as the most fundamental moral principle of all, as it "comprehends every rule of justice without exception" (AP, 275).

> In every case, we ought to act that part towards another, which we would judge to be right in him to act toward us, if we were in his circumstances and he in ours; or more generally—What we approve in others, that we ought to practise in like circumstances, and what we condemn in others we ought not to do. (AP, 274)

This is a principle of *impartiality*—not only a requirement of logical consistency but also a requirement of fairness, or justice—one that respects the moral standing of each individual agent.

Not only does Reid think that this sort of impartiality is necessary for moral judgment in general but it also has special importance for judgments concerning favor, justice, and injury. For someone's resentment at being injured by another to rise to the level of moral judgment, it must be implicitly general. That is, if it is appropriate for me to resent being treated a certain way, it is appropriate for anyone else who suffers similar treatment to feel the same way.

But *I* need not be the one who is wronged in order to feel resentment. Butler calls resentment on behalf of others *indignation*:

> The indignation raised by cruelty and injustice, and the desire of having it punished, which persons unconcerned would feel, is by no means malice. No, it is resentment against vice and wickedness: it is one of the common bonds, by which society is held together; a fellow-feeling, which each individual has in behalf of the whole species, as well as of himself. (Butler, 129–130)

However, it is crucial to notice that this is not merely indignation at someone for acting contrary to public utility (a wrong *to the public*). Rather, as we have noted with Smith, the focus remains on those *individuals* who have been injured and the agents responsible for causing their injury. The generality of the response, then, is that one's resentment can have as its proper object injury to *anyone*. One might also be angered by attacks on public utility as such, but this is distinct from being moved directly by the plight of the specific injured party.

Occasionally Hume makes passing reference to private wrongs as distinct from harms to public utility, but he pays surprisingly little attention to this when talking about justice. Reid is struck by Hume's restriction of justice to property and the keeping of contracts, noting that Hume simply remains silent on the other branches of justice. However, Reid adds:

> He no where says, that it is not naturally criminal to rob an innocent man of his life, of his children, of his liberty, or of his reputation; and I am apt to think he never meant it. (AP, 315)

But if Hume were to agree that this was merely an oversight on his part, Reid would press his point all the further:

> No man would allow him to be a man of honour, who should plead his interest to justify what he acknowledged to be dishonourable; but to sacrifice interest to honour never costs a blush. (AP, 170)

What must be recalled is that Hume's sensible knave is inviting us to consider an *act of iniquity or infidelity*. Such "thoughts of villainy or baseness," says Hume, are repulsive to the heart of an honest person. But, to understand this, it is essential that we focus on the injured party. That is, this is first and foremost a *private injury* rather than an injury to the public interest.

What sort of private injury is it? Reid maintains that it is an act of *injustice* against the injured party. It violates, as Reid would put it, "the right of an innocent man to the safety of his person and [perhaps to his] family, to his liberty and reputation" (AP, 656). Without acknowledging this, it is not clear to Reid how the voice of justice can be fully heard. However, by acknowledging it, Reid insists, Hume must concede that there are at least some branches of justice that are not derived solely from public utility.

So, an important consequence of Reid's insistence that justice is not derived solely from public utility is that space is provided for a more satisfying response to the sensible knave. A "feeling of the heart" can, indeed, arise "from the judgment of [one's] understanding"—an understanding that one who acts as the sensible knave proposes is causing private injury to specific persons, whether oneself or others. This, Smith and Reid maintain, warrants resentment, or indignation. Of course, if the number of sensible knaves were to grow large enough, this could cause a "considerable breach in the social union and confederacy;" but that would be an *additional* injury to those already caused by the individual acts of "iniquity or infidelity" the sensible knave favors. A sensible knave may not be moved by this. However, for a "man of honour" (Reid) or those with an "ingenuous nature" (Hume), "the antipathy to treachery and roguery is too strong to be counterbalanced by any views of profit or pecuniary advantage"—or, if Reid is right, perhaps even by views of public utility. As Reid and Smith (as well as Butler) acknowledge, justice does serve public utility, but it serves other equally important moral ends as well.

In fact, Reid is willing to acknowledge an obligation to support justice that is based on its tendency to support public utility. However, he adds:

> To perceive that justice tends to the good of mankind, would lay no moral obligation upon us to be just, unless we be conscious of a moral obligation to do what tends to the good of mankind. If such a moral obligation be admitted, *why may we not admit a stronger obligation to do injury to no man?* The last obligation is as easily conceived as the first, and there is as clear evidence of its existence in human nature. (AP, 326)

For both Reid and Smith it is important to distinguish the *consequences* of one's resentment from its *object*. As Smith puts it:

> What chiefly enrages us against the man who injures or insults us, is the little account which he seems to make of us, the unreasonable preference which he gives to himself above us, and that absurd self-love, by which he seems to imagine, that other people may be sacrificed at any time, to his conveniency or his humour. (TMS, 96)

Although the sensible knave may take care not to harm the public good or his own self-interest, he cannot escape this criticism. Furthermore, this criticism is grounded in resentment insofar as it is constrained by the inner voice of the impartial spectator.

Smith points out that the perspective of the impartial spectator does not oppose partiality to oneself or to one's "near and dear" as such. It only insists that this be constrained by considerations of justice:

> There can be no proper motive for hurting our neighbour, there can be no incitement to do evil to another, which mankind will go along with, except just indignation for evil which that other has done to us. To disturb his happiness merely because it stands in the way of our own, to take from him what is of real use to him merely because it may be of equal or of more use to us, or to indulge, in this manner, at the expence of other people, the natural preference which every man has for his own happiness above that of other people, is what no impartial spectator can go along with. (TMS, 82)

For Smith, the sensible knave will not be well received by those with the self-command of an impartial spectator. This is because, even though the sensible knave will try to avoid undermining the public good, he is prepared to commit acts of iniquity at the expense of others when it seems to be to his advantage. In contrast, someone with the virtue of firm self-command

> does not merely affect the sentiments of the impartial spectator. He really adopts them. He almost identifies himself with, he almost becomes himself that impartial spectator, and scarce even feels but as that great arbiter of his conduct directs him to feel. (TMS, 147)

The indignation that the knave's acts of iniquity and dishonesty give rise to expresses a central moral value of those with self-command. As Smith says:

> One individual must never prefer himself so much even to any other individual, as to hurt or injure that other, in order to benefit himself, though the benefit to the one should be much greater than the hurt or injury to the other. (TMS, 138)

The sensible knave is quite prepared to ignore this when he is convinced he can get away with making himself an exception to the rule.

The sensible knave does recognize the need for rules of justice that serve public utility. He sees the importance of *appearing* to be an advocate of such rules. He also sees the importance of not actually threatening the security of society when he (secretly) violates these rules. Finally, he understands the importance of actually being the gainer by violating these rules. (He must see himself as really being "the exception who proves the rules").

So, do the sensible knave's "sensible" features line up well with common sense and reason? Such a knave is seriously committed to supporting his short-term and long-term personal interests. Sensibly pursuing such ends certainly requires reason. Does it also require common sense? To a large extent, there is a match between what common sense supports and the personal gain sought by a sensible knave. However, making oneself the exception to the rules of common sense is not something supported by the common sense's sharable, public test of acceptability.

Smith's notion of an impartial spectator provides a guide for how reason can respond to the sensible knave. In his discussion of fair competition Smith says that if one resort to "jostling" an opponent, this is a violation of rules that others will not allow as fair. But this seems to be precisely what the sensible knave is up to (or would be if he thought he could get away with it). This kind of act may or may not pose a threat to public utility. But the wrong is done to the victim and must be acknowledged as such. The hypothesis is that the sensible knave is guarding against causing any significant public harm (vs. public utility). But it is not part of this hypothesis that no significant injury is (or could be) caused to the victim, and it is this that Smith holds we should not lose sight of in appraising the sensible knave's posture.

What is the public assessment of the knave's perspective? Here Smith's response seems much more refined than Hume's. Smith objects to anyone who "jostles" another with whom he is engaged in competition. This, he says, is unfair and will not be tolerated (if known) by others. *This* is the objection to the knave who is willing to cheat, steal, etc. in order to get ahead. He is willing to trade his integrity for "worthless gews and gee-gaws." This is a moral wronging of victim and a moral diminishment of the knave.

So, even if the sensible knave is *rational*, he does not accept the demands of being *reasonable*. Is this a *rational* shortcoming or a deficiency of *sentiment*? It certainly involves the latter. But it is essential to realize that this deficiency of sentiment also betrays a moral shortcoming in the use of *reason*. This will be evident when Reid's "law of the prophets" is brought to bear on the sensible knave's. As we have seen, the "law of the prophets" requires the fully *reciprocal* use of the principle—not simply a one-sided (when favorable to me) use.

The sensible knave is differently motivated in his knavish employment of reason. So his sentiments are different from others. He seems not to be invested in any concern to maintain his moral integrity. Instead, the sensible knave is concerned to employ reason in service of his self-interest exclusive of any interest in doing what morality as such requires. A concern for one's *integrity* engages reason more comprehensively than that employed by the sensible knave. The *common* sense of those who enter into moral disputes demands more than the sensibility and practical reason the knave has to offer.

Hume says his account of morality is one that is "founded entirely on the particular fabric and constitution of the human species" (ECM, 74)— one that perhaps "depends on some internal sense of feeling, which nature has made universal in the whole species" (ECM, 74). Like moral beauty, Hume adds, it "demands the assistance of our intellectual faculties, in order to give it a suitable influence on the human mind" (ECM, 76). As in the case of beauty in the finer arts, "it is requisite to employ much reasoning, in order to feel the proper sentiment; and a false relish may frequently be corrected by argument and reflection" (ECM, 76). Unfortunately, Hume does not offer detailed illustrations of reasoning at work in this way in either his *Enquiry* or *Treatise*.

In contrast, Reid does offer a number of illustrations of how he thinks practical reason works in morality, particularly in his discussion of Butler's subtle treatment of the various forms of resentment. (Smith, too, offers such a detailed discussion of resentment in his *Theory of Moral Sentiments*.) Oddly, despite his familiarity with and admiration of his writings, Hume did not discuss Butler's account of resentment. This was a missed opportunity, one that invited him to join Reid and Smith in discussing the moral development of children.

Fundamental to Reid's account of morality is that not all creatures capable of being moved by desires and sentiments fall under the umbrella of moral agency. This is why he spends so much time distinguishing what he calls animal from rational principles of action. "Clever" as they might appear to be, foxes cannot be sensible knaves. Humans, however, from infancy forward, have the makings of becoming moral agents—and of knavery. That is, an infant has what Reid calls "the seeds of morality." Telling a plausible story about these seeds of morality is crucial to giving an account of the basic features of morality (and moral agency). However, for Reid (and presumably Hume and Smith as well), no such story about a baby fox can even begin.

Hume attempts to show how justice's moral importance is derived from its contribution to public utility. However, public utility is not a notion that can be grasped by a fox. It neither possesses nor has the capacity to possess such a concept. Nor does it have the capacity to grasp Reid's "law of the prophets" (or Smith's notion of an impartial spectator). For Reid, this "law of the prophets" is the *sine qua non* of moral agency. If it is not grasped (and appreciated), we have no moral agent. This is the principle that expresses a fundamental feature of generality of morality for Reid.

When Hume appeals to morality's generality, he refers to a shared *sentiment of humanity* that extols dispositions such as beneficence, kindness, and compassion, which are met with approval by virtually everyone everywhere. Each of these dispositions can be found to some extent in virtually everyone, Hume thinks, and collectively they support public utility.

However, neither Reid nor Hume's account applies to a fox or a mouse. A fox may "steal" a farmer's chicken, but without seeing this as "theft." A mouse may be lured by cheese into a mousetrap. But if it is successful in avoiding the dangers of the trap, it doesn't do so by conceptualizing the trap (or situation) in moral terms. In contrast, a sensible knave deliberately uses verbal and other forms of deception to avoid being caught and to maintain his reputation of being morally upright and trustworthy.

In short, the sensible knave, too, must go through a social development process. However, obviously, not everything that factors into the development of an ordinary person's conscience has a similar impact on someone who would become a full-fledged knave. Knaves who are less than sensible not only lack the relevant sentiments, but they also lack the fuller implementation of reason found in more sensible knaves. A successful knave needs cleverness, patience, insight, and farsightedness, all of which require the use of reason.

Like Hume, Smith insists that the right kinds of sentiments are the marks of morality. But he appeals to the idea of an "impartial spectator" in searching for a principle from which we can reason in common. As his *Theory of the Moral Sentiments* amply illustrates, this searching requires the employment of reason.

Reid's "law of the prophets," too, requires the use of reason in its insistence that a moral agent must employ the sort of reciprocal thinking that judges relevantly similar cases similarly, regardless of to whom this judging applies. This opposes the kind of thinking the sensible knave uses in making himself an exception to the rules. By his own admission, he does not operate with a "principle from which we can reason in common."

Reid and Smith morally object to the *knavishness* of the sensible knave. The knave fails to show appropriate respect for his victim. He is considering only his own (apparent) advantage. Although both Reid and Smith agree with the idea that some partiality toward oneself and one's "near and dear" is natural and acceptable, they also agree that the sensible knave goes too far in his partiality to himself. This "jostling" (cheating, or rule-breaking), as Smith puts it, is not something that others find acceptable. It is this that Smith finds morally unacceptable about the knave's willingness to make himself an exception to the rules. To a large extent, his *Theory of the Moral Sentiments* articulates the nature of this objection and the difficulties in fully attaining the moral perspective it expresses.

Chapter 5

THE PREMISE OF A PROMISE

We have seen that Thomas Reid credits even young children with a solid understanding of promises and the obligations they entail. Recall his example of the two boys playing with a top and scourge. Let's continue this story for Reid. Suppose the top belongs to Calvin, the scourge to Andy. Calvin takes the first turn. When the top stops spinning, Calvin hands the scourge back to Andy, picks up his top and abruptly leaves. "But you *promised*," says Andy. Absent some special explanation or apology, both boys should agree that a wrong has been done. Not only is Andy disappointed at not having his turn with the top, seemingly the trust he extended to Calvin was *betrayed*—Calvin had *given his word*.

What else needs to be added to this story for us to understand what has happened and why the boys should see it as morally problematic? For Reid, very little, if anything. The mutual promise made by the boys is understood by both to have committed them knowingly and willingly to take turns. But this is likely not the only communication between them. For example, Calvin might also have indicated to Andy that he was going to an event with his parents that evening. But this would not be a promise of anything to Andy. It may suggest that Calvin believes he has an obligation to be with his parents that evening. However, Calvin's departure without offering any explanation parting words need not call this to mind. To all appearances, Calvin simply broke his promise to Andy.

Clearly, Calvin and Andy know how to promise, and they can recognize when a promise has been made to them. They both know that Calvin's breaking his promise without any explanation or indication that he will make up for this later is morally problematic. This story, we could say, presents us with *the premise of a promise*.[1] This premise does not include a definition

---

1 In response to my question, "Why should one keep one's promises?", my late first wife, Millie, once said, without any hesitation: "It's the premise of a promise." She offered no elaboration, holding that this is all that needs to be said. In effect, I think Reid would agree.

of "contract" or "promise." It does not presume or rely on an underlying, elaborate theory of promising. It includes only the boys' *understanding* of what has taken place. Calvin and Andy promised each other and thereby took on obligations to each other.

But, asks David Hume, what does this really come to? What sort of *act of mind* is this promising? It cannot simply be a matter of *resolving* to do something. I can resolve to myself that I will do something. I can even say out loud to others that I have resolved to do something. But such a resolution is not a promise to one another. *Desiring* to do something does not suffice either. I can say out loud to others that I desire to do something. But, as such, this does not bring about the obligation to keep a promise either.

Can I somehow *will* an obligation? Yes, says Reid, by promising. No, says Hume, an obligation requires a special *sentiment*. Not only is there no natural sentiment to keep one's promises, but we also cannot simply will a sentiment into existence. So, Hume concludes that there is a difficulty in explaining the obligation of promises. In the end, he says, we must somehow *feign* an act of mind that is, strictly speaking, impossible.

To this Reid objects:

> The obligation of Contracts and Promises is a matter so sacred, and of such consequence to human society, that speculations which have a tendency to weaken that obligation, and to perplex men's notions on a subject so plain and so important, ought to meet with the disapprobation of all honest men. (AP, 663)

He concludes that Hume's account is needlessly complicated in ways that threaten our confidence in promising straightforwardly creating obligations. The key to the simpler story Reid offers is his distinction between *solitary* and *social* acts of the mind. It is, Reid thinks, Hume's failure fully to appreciate the distinctiveness of *social* acts of the mind that leads him astray. A social act of mind is one that, at least in its central instances, *requires* communication with others. I might reveal to others that I have a pain in my arm, but I can keep this to myself. The pain is there in either case. But *giving testimony* or *asking*, for example, presuppose a social context in which communication with others is an essential feature of how we are to understand the act in question. *Promising*, too, is a social act—communicating that one is voluntarily taking on an obligation to another. In cases like that of Andy and Calvin, the understanding is mutual—they are *in agreement*. This agreement is made possible because both Andy and Calvin understand (even without being able to define) what promising is and, most importantly, what the signs of promise-making are. In this way, the act of promising does will an obligation.

Even in the absence of resolve, desire, or sentiment, someone who promises is understood to have taken on an obligation. In fact, even lying promises are, nevertheless, binding. They are social acts that attempt to deceive others by trying to fool others into counting on them to keep their word—to fulfill the promise. But promises they are. One cannot undo the *social* features of such acts by silent denial of the sincerity of one's word. Whether or not one's promise is made with sincerity is irrelevant. On Reid's account, no special desire or sentiment is necessary for there to be a resulting obligation.

Hume's account of the basis of the obligation of promising has strong similarities to his discussion of justice in his *Enquiry Concerning the Principles of Morals*, which focuses on the public utility of respecting rules about property. He claims that the sentiments related to justice are derived either from our reflecting on the tendency of justice to promote public utility or from some "simple original instinct, and is not ascertained by any argument or reflection." He quickly rejects the second alternative. This leaves him with the task of explaining the sentiments of justice in relation to their contribution to public utility. Similarly, how one should regard promises is grounded in the recognition of the public utility resulting from the general practice of promise making and promise keeping.

In contrast, although Reid agrees that respect for the general practice of promising does serve public utility, he offers a different account of acts of promising themselves. This is illustrated in his example of the two boys playing with the top and scourge. Given their mutual promise, when Calvin abruptly returns Andy's scourge, picks up his top, and leaves, Andy might well be angered. In line with Butler, Reid would say that this anger is a form of *resentment*.

Could Andy's resentment be a "simple original instinct" that is not ascertained by argument or reflection? Although Hume's list of such instincts includes resentment, he does not characterize any items on this list as *moral* sentiments. Instinctive resentment is Butler's "sudden resentment," a defensive response that we share with nonhuman animals, and which has no distinctively moral features. *Moral* approval and disapproval must meet a test of *generality*. For Hume, the "simple original instinct" that eventually gets generalized into a moral sentiment is *benevolence*, thus underlining the importance of its public utility. Although he nowhere discusses resentment at any length, were Hume to do so, it is likely that he would insist that, like benevolence, whatever generalization might be associated with it must also be linked to its public utility. But, given its negative qualities, it would not fare as well as benevolence.

In response, Reid insists that there is an important distinction *within morality* between resentment at private injury and resentment at injury to the public; and, he suggests, it is Hume's apparent failure to fully appreciate this distinction that gets in the way of seeing that justice need not be derived from utility. (This is Smith's view, as well. But, unlike Reid, Smith does not explicitly mention Hume in presenting it.) Like Hume, Reid insists that moral sentiments presume a dimension of generality that the "simple original instincts" of benevolence and resentment lack. However, generality in morality for Reid comes from something other than the notion of public utility. It comes from a principle that "comprehends every rule of justice without exception":

> In every case, we ought to act that part towards another, which we would judge to be right in him to act toward us, if we were in his circumstances and he in ours; or more generally—What we approve in others, that we ought to practise in like circumstances and what we condemn in others we ought not to do. (AP, 274)

This is a principle of *impartiality* in judgment—a requirement of consistency that is also a requirement of fairness, or justice.

Even if Hume's notion of public utility actually were to include acceptance of this principle of impartiality of judgment, Reid's principle of justice can be understood and acted on quite independently of considerations of public utility. In fact, Reid believes that for most people, most of the time, concern for public utility does not underlie their concerns about justice. However, he insists, acceptance of the principle of impartiality is a necessary condition for being a moral agent at all: "If a man is not capable of perceiving this in his cool moments, when he reflects seriously, he is not a moral agent, nor is he capable of being convinced of it by reasoning" (AP, 177).

So, is Andy's resentment a *moral* sentiment? Reid would be convinced that it is, provided that, if the roles were reversed, Andy would agree that he would be wronging Calvin if he left without allowing him his turn.

In their assessment of *practical* affairs, Hume and Reid actually have much in common. They both accept the following:

- The stability and viability of society depend on the maintenance of the practice of promising, a practice in which those who make promises believe themselves to be taking on obligations to do what they promise.
- This practice can be maintained only if those who make promises can, for the most part, be trusted to keep their word.
- The maintenance of a stable and viable society is in everyone's interest.
- The expectation of personal gain from making and keeping promises can be a powerful motive for keeping our promises.
- The fear of discovery and consequent loss of the trust of others can be a powerful motive for keeping our promises.

However, as discussed in Chapter 4, Hume invites us to consider the challenge of a "sensible knave." Such a knave can accept all of the above, but still wonder whether there might not be "exceptions to the rule" in his favor.

It is in everyone's interest, including the knave's, that sensible knavery in others be discouraged. For Reid, it seems obvious both that we have an obligation to keep our promises, as well as what the basis of that obligation is. Understanding and supporting the obligation of promises is so important that, as already noted, Reid says, "speculations which have a tendency to weaken that obligation, and to perplex men's notions on a subject so plain and so important, ought to meet with the disapprobation of all honest men" (AP, 663).

The speculations Reid has foremost in mind are those of Hume. Reid says that it is Hume's ideas that meet with his disapproval, not Hume the person. He is convinced that Hume is as *practically* committed to the obligation of promises as anyone. The problem is that Hume's *philosophical* account of that obligation needlessly complicates "a subject so plain." Given the importance of the subject, Reid thinks that Hume's view is not only philosophically mistaken, but it may also be practically dangerous.

Since Hume's explicit discussion of justice is confined to property, his taxonomy differs significantly from Reid's. However, Hume's discussion of the obligation of promises resembles his discussion of justice in fundamental ways. The sensible knave still poses a problem after Hume has completed his account of the derivation of justice from utility. Although the sensible knave appreciates the advantages rules of justice provide him, he "may think that an act of iniquity or infidelity will make a considerable addition to his fortune, without causing any considerable breach in the social union and confederacy" (EM, 282).

The obligation to keep promises seems similarly challenged by the sensible knave. The knave can acknowledge that, in general, he stands much to gain if he keeps his promises, and he risks much if he is caught breaking his promises. Furthermore, he can acknowledge that observance of the general rule that we should keep our promises serves public utility. Still, he reasons that there are some occasions when breaking a promise is to his personal advantage and that this will not cause "any considerable breach in the social union and confederacy."

It is plausible to conclude that Hume's response to the sensible knave's challenge to promise-keeping would be the same as his response to the challenge to justice. As seen in Chapter 4, Hume replies to this challenge by making an appeal to conscience—the ordinary person's, not the sensible knave's. Reid agrees with an appeal to conscience in opposition to the sensible knave's conduct, but he thinks that this is not restricted to considerations of public utility. Reid's dissatisfaction with Hume's account of promising is similar.

In his attempt to prove that there is no *natural* obligation to keep one's promises, Hume essentially argues that children (and adults) have strong knavish tendencies. This is moderated somewhat by mutual affection among family and friends and by "natural instincts" of kindness, benevolence, and resentment toward those with whom we are largely unacquainted. However, insofar as they operate outside the circle of intimates, these "natural instincts" are irregular and inconstant. None of this is sufficient to sustain promising in the larger area of society that depends on it for "interested commerce." There is a fundamental question of how to establish sufficient trust among strangers so that the benefits of "interested commerce" can be obtained.

For Hume, as children develop their rational capacities, it may be expected that eventually they will acquire the understanding of the importance of promising as an instrument of utility enabling society to function smoothly and productively. They will also understand how, as individuals, promising enables them to gain for themselves goods and services they could not have without the cooperation of others.

But what are the mechanisms that make possible this understanding and appreciation of the obligation of promises? And is this enough? What makes this possible is the combination of our natural interests (largely, but not exclusively, in satisfying what we want for ourselves) with the realization that large-scale cooperation is necessary to succeed in fulfilling them. Promising is one way to secure cooperation. But this requires sufficient trust between people that, under certain circumstances (such as promising), we are willing to rely on others to provide the goods and services we want at a later date. That is, we accept their promises to perform tasks in the future. For Hume, we come to appreciate this both at the level of individual interaction and at the level of overall utility to society. From the perspective of the sensible knave, the expectation of personal benefit and the fear of loss of trust oblige us (practically, not morally) to keep our promises—and this is further reinforced as we see that this practice is essential to the larger society we depend on as well.

But how is this practice to be established in the first place? Here is where Hume thinks that human *inventiveness* is required. To get past the sensible knave's position, we must come to see ourselves *as if*, by an *act of willing*, we create an obligation. But, as there is no natural act of mind that can accomplish this, it is necessary to *feign* an act of mind in a way that *convinces* both ourselves and others that we have created an obligation simply by indicating that we are taking on this obligation.

So, it seems, we act *as if* we are creating this obligation, and we *believe* we are doing so simply by willing the obligation by an act of mind. But if we are philosophically clear-headed about this, we will see that there really is no act of mind that has the power to create an obligation (just as, Hume says, transubstantiation is a myth). In short, when we turn to philosophy, we will see that what we take to be "natural" is really "artificial," and rather than strengthening the hold of the obligation of promises, realizing this, Reid might say, can risk weakening it. For him, this is both philosophically and practically unacceptable. But, he is convinced that a better philosophical account is available. The question, Reid might ask, is whether there really is an obligation created by the *feigning* allegedly involved in promising. This practice doesn't make the imagined obligation any more "real" than anything else. All that Hume has offered is an explanation of how we have come to *accept* the idea that there is an obligation. Reid offers us a different explanation—one that he believes is closer to our everyday understanding of promising.

Reid's claim is that young children understand promising and accept the idea of obligation that goes with it long before they can tell Hume's story about the usefulness of promising for society. In fact, Reid says, the average person seldom, if ever, thinks about promising in the way Hume describes.

Hume's account of how we've come to accept the bindingness of promises goes something like this: We begin with admittedly knavish tendencies (along with occasional, but irregular, natural sentiments of benevolence). As we develop our prudential understanding, first we see the advantage of promising in order to get what we want (on an individual level); later we see the advantage of having a practice that is widespread throughout society. In order to make all of this work, we *feign* an act of mind (creating an obligation through promising).

But, this story does not work well. The first promises children succeed in making will need somehow to involve the *feigning* Hume posits. However, either children realize that this is only a feigning, in which case they don't really believe an obligation is created, or children don't think of it as feigning at all. On Hume's account, children at least realize that it is important to keep their promises in order to sustain the trust that is necessary for "promising" to obligate. So, they have an expectation of getting something (though promising) that it would have been more difficult to get without promising, and they have an incentive to keep their promises in order to be trusted the next time they promise. None of this requires children to have an understanding of the utility of promising for society as a whole—nor an understanding of the importance of a stable/effective society for everyone's well-being.

Still, nothing yet indicates that children have an understanding of the *obligation* of promises as this is ordinarily understood—and as Hume wants it to be understood by adults. So far, we simply have children who may be, for all we may know, on the way to sensible knavery.

The question is this: How are we to explain the alleged *feigning* that Hume's posits? When is one capable of this and why would one engage in such an act of mind? Most of us are not sensible knaves, according to both Hume and Reid. It seems that, at some point, the *feigning* must begin—but without a realization on the part of the individual that *this* is what is going on. If the feigning is deliberate and self-conscious, it would seem that we may simply have the makings of a sensible knave.

Reid's view is that our ability to understand promising develops very early in life. Promising is "natural," at least in the sense that understanding the *bindingness* of promises does not require any understanding of the utility of promising for society. It is Reid's view that even adults seldom, if ever, consider the general utility of promise making and promise keeping. Further, Reid would say that understanding the obligation of promises does not *depend* on a realization that promising-making serves one's self-interest (or that promise-breaking threatens it). This realization is likely to be there, but so is something else—namely the capacity to recognize *natural signs* of promising. An environment of *trust* and *fidelity* with others may be necessary for this capacity to mature into understanding and commitment. And it is possible that, for most, such an environment will not be present without a larger society that has an established practice of promising. But even if these *causal* dependencies are there, it does not follow that the idea of justice, and promising, is derived solely from considerations of public utility.

In fact, Reid could argue, without the capacity for promising, neither trust among individuals nor across a society could become established. Reid's point is that the capacity to promise (and take oneself to have thereby created an obligation) is a part of our natural constitution. This differentiates us from other species. Although we have much in common with nonhuman animals ("brute animals"), Reid says:

> They can neither plight their veracity by testimony nor their fidelity by any engagement or promise [...].
>   A fox is said to use stratagems, but he cannot lie, because he cannot give his testimony, or plight his veracity. A dog is said to be faithful to his master; but no more is meant but that he is affectionate, for he never came under any engagement [...]. (AP, 664)

Reid acknowledges that we are not born with an understanding of promising, but he does insist that our initial understanding is not acquired through reasoning or instruction. Rather, it is through the perception of *natural signs* that this understanding is acquired. Nonhumans perceive many of the natural signs that we do (e.g., signs of anger, threats). However, there are natural signs that only humans can understand. In regard to promises, it is necessary first that children establish bonds of trust and fidelity with others. This, Reid says, has its beginnings in infancy: "[...] it is a certain fact, that we can perceive some communication of sentiments between the nurse and her nursling, before it is a month old." (AP, 664) Furthermore, although a viable society does depend on widespread understanding and acceptance of the practice of promising, we are so *naturally constituted* that, given a socially nurturing environment, the good faith and trust that eventually lead to an understanding of promising will emerge in the child: "[...] good faith on the one part and trust on the other—are formed by nature in the minds of children, before they are capable of knowing their utility, or being influenced by considerations either of duty or interest" (AP, 666).

So, very young children develop the ability to promise. Now, does it matter whether we call this the ability to *feign*, as distinct from *really* create, an obligation? Hume denies that promising creates a new sentiment. Reid can agree. This would simply reinforce his view that, important as sentiment (including "natural" sentiment) is for morality, morality is not simply a matter of sentiment. In fact, Reid claims, morality is also a matter of establishing relationships with others by *expressing one's will* to others in ways that affect others' expectations—and which warrant various responses when trust/ fidelity is sustained and when it is breached.

At some point, we must move to a *normative* account in all of this. Reid is trying to characterize normative discourse and communication. We live *inside* this discourse and communication. Hume tries to view it from outside and give an account of what is "really" happening when we promise. Then, when faced with the sensible knave, he tries to get back inside (by appealing to one's integrity in responding to the sensible knave). Reid refuses to step outside our everyday understandings. Is he a "realist" when it comes to obligations? Well, he isn't a reductionist. Like Hume, he consistently resists "reducing" obligation to such states of mind as resolutions and desires. He submits that his account is more faithful to our understanding of ourselves as moral agents with moral concerns than Hume's.

Here is where Reid's distinction between *individual* and *social* acts of the mind is of crucial importance. By moving to social understandings (that are "natural"), Reid moves into the realm of normative concern. Promising is itself an act of mind that is social, not solitary. It cannot be defined, but (like seeing, hearing, remembering, imagining, smelling) it can be understood without being defined. We understand that seeing and hearing are different, that remembering and imagining are different, that smelling and remembering a smell are different—and that resolving is different from promising and that desiring is different from promising. In contrast to resolving and desiring, promising is *social* in ways that resolving and desiring need not be.

What Hume lacks, Reid might say, is an adequate account of *communication and social understanding*. The building blocks of communication with others are present in the nursery—as it is here that we find the beginnings of trust and fidelity that will enable the infant to develop into a child who will be able to make truly binding promises.

Chapter 6

CONVERSATION AND CRITICAL THINKING

In discussing effective means of regulating the sentiments and the behavior associated with them, Adam Smith emphasized the importance of conversation:

> Society and conversation are the most powerful remedies for restoring the mind to its tranquility, if at any time, it has unfortunately lost it; as well as the best preservatives of that equal and happy temper which is so necessary to self-satisfaction and enjoyment. (TMS, 23)

This emphasis on the importance of conversation fits in well with Smith's account of the moral development of children, especially insofar as it focuses on the socialization of children outside the immediate confines of the home. Smith does not provide details of how moral conversation among children might go. However, this chapter offers an extended sample from conversations I have had with a group of students with whom I had a number of meetings beginning when they were 10- to 11-year-old 5th graders.

I met weekly with this group some years ago in an after-school program during the regular school year. For our last session, we discussed ideas related to reciprocity. Although the word "reciprocity" was not used in that conversation (or in any of our previous ones), it was the basic notion under consideration in this final session.[1]

In one guise or another, reciprocity is commonly regarded to be a fundamental moral value. For example, it is a pivotal notion moral and religious traditions that invoke some form of the Golden Rule. In the case of Thomas Reid, some understanding and acceptance of reciprocity is a necessary condition for being a moral agent. It is also at the heart of Adam

---

1 The full transcript of this conversation was first published in my *Philosophical Adventures with Children* (University Press of America, 1985). Substantial portions of that conversation are included here. Unfortunately, this book is now out of print; but its examples of children's conversations retain their relevance today.

Smith's notion of an "impartial spectator." Reciprocity can take on many forms. For example, in social relations reciprocity might be understood generally as "returning in kind." But this could include concerns as various as a fair exchange of goods, paying one's debts, returning favors, wanting to "get even," or trying to teach someone a lesson.

Sessions with my group of 5th graders typically began with a reading and discussion of short passages from Matthew Lipman's *Harry Stottlemeier's Discovery* and further ideas to which this gave rise. However, often we were still in the heat of discussion when it was time for a session to conclude. This prompted a return next time to unresolved matters from the previous week in light of the group's further reflections. Among the many topics discussed were: good and bad reasoning; what should count as evidence; what are good reasons for believing something; what counts as proof; relationships among minds, brains, and computers; relationships between dreams and waking states; the extent to which we can know who we really are; and what we can learn from thinking about how we think.

Our regular meeting place was an unadorned room in the Ransom Public Library, located in the small town of Plainwell, Michigan. However, for our last session, we accepted an invitation to travel 12 miles to Western Michigan University in Kalamazoo, where our discussion would be videotaped. Gone was our private, cozy room in the library. In its place was a large studio complete with floodlights, several cameras, a microphone hanging from a boom, and a lot of complex gadgetry—all of which threatened to present an intimidating atmosphere for a group of fifth graders.

My first task was to pick something promising for discussion. I selected an episode in Matthew Lipman's novel *Lisa*, the sequel to *Harry*. We had not read this episode in advance of our session. Harry and Timmy go to a stamp club where postage stamps are traded. Then they go to an ice cream parlor. But Timmy has no money. So, Harry offers to buy Timmy a cone. Timmy accepts, indicating that he will buy next time. As they are leaving, another child deliberately trips Timmy, who responds by knocking the tripper's books off his table. Then Harry and Timmy run out of the store and down the street. Later Timmy says that he had to knock the books off the table—he couldn't just let the other boy get away with tripping him. He concludes that he had to try to get even with him.

I then invited comments about Timmy's handling of the situation. Carlen offered her thoughts:

> CARLEN: Sometimes if you were to do things back to them, then they would want to do it back to you, and it just turns out that it gets worse and worse. So, maybe it's better just to forget about it and let him [the tripper] be the child and think that he shouldn't have done it.

CHIP: Well, sometimes when somebody does something to you to make you mad and you don't even think about it or anything like that, then it's no fun for them, and it just ruins their play. That's what they wanted to do.

KURT: Well, if you keep letting them push you around and stuff, then they grow up to be like that and then if they used to be buddies, you may not be buddies when you grow up, and it wouldn't be so good.

PRITCHARD: So, which side are you on, Kurt? Do you think that what Timmy did was maybe okay—or not okay?

KURT: Yeah, it was okay.

RICK: It's okay to do something to somebody if it's a nice thing and have them do it back to you; but two wrongs don't make a right.

PRITCHARD: So, you think the difference here is that what Timmy did wasn't really nice, and what happened to him wasn't nice, but the trading of stamps and buying the ice cream cone—those were nice?

RICK: Well, I guess it's something nice, and [...] it's a pretty good deed to do something back to him that's nice. But if it's just something wrong, then it's not a very good idea.

EMILY: I think if somebody trips me I would just walk away and just ignore the person, because [...] what the person really wants is attention and his friends to laugh at him and stuff like that. So I would just walk away and not do anything.

PENNY: I agree with Emily. It would be better to walk away, because if [...] you push off his books, well, he was probably expecting it, because he knew that bothered you. So, if he knew you'd try to every time he saw you, he'd probably try to trip you. So if you just walked away, then he wouldn't think it bothered you.

CARLEN: I can see how Timmy *wanted* to throw his books off because he could get you really mad. But you have to be able to ignore it and be able not to do it, [...].

LARRY: Well, I think he should start with the problem and tell the kid to leave you alone, because you didn't do anything to him, and he had no reason to trip you. So you should just tell him to leave you alone. That'll be the end of it, [...] maybe, [...] unless the kid sees that he can get a rise out of you and he just keeps on, you know, pushing farther and farther. Sometimes you do need to get even. Well, actually, there's no such thing as even, because then he'll get even.

PRITCHARD: So, what does it mean when we say, "I had to get even"? Does it really make any sense?

LARRY: He didn't have to. He *wanted* to, but he didn't *have* to.

I had not expected Larry's answer. I thought he might say a bit more about his view that "there's no such thing as even," since each person will keep on trying to "even the score." But Larry made a new, and equally important, point. He made a distinction between what one *has* to do and what one *wants* to do. By challenging the claim that one must try to get even, Larry seemed to be suggesting that one cannot easily avoid responsibility for one's actions. Chip continued:

> CHIP: He wanted to get even because lots of times you walk around with a friend and somebody does something to you and you would think that if you didn't get even with him, then your friends would make fun of you or something like that.
>
> CARLEN: I don't think I would do what Larry said, just walk by after he tripped you and say, "Stop it" in a real sassy way, because he might think that that's a way of getting attention and he would do it again.
>
> LARRY: Well, I was saying just ask nicely or [...] ask him why he did it or ask him if he needs attention or something, and he'll leave you alone.
>
> KURT: I don't think so.
>
> PRITCHARD: You don't think so, Kurt?
>
> KURT: No, because people like that, they don't just give up on one little thing. They just keep doing it until they kind of get in big trouble.

In trying to determine what to do, the students clearly recognized the importance of considering both the reasons why another might engage in aggressive behavior as well as the possible consequences of responding to that aggression in one way rather than another. They also reflected on the question of what would be the *right* course of action.

I raised the question of how Timmy's response to being tripped differed from Harry buying an ice cream cone for Timmy:

> JEFF: Well, you're not hurting anybody when you buy them an ice cream cone [...]. Like, if someone buys you an ice cream cone, then you say you'll repay them and buy them. Then they'll buy you one. Well, it's okay to do that. But if somebody hurts you, well, then it's not really right to go back and hit them.
>
> EMILY: Like, for that kind of thing, a person is giving you something that you can use, and you need; and that's a nice thing to do, and you should do something nice to that person to repay them. But, like, the only time you should hit a person if they hit you is only to defend yourself—not to get even with the person.

PRITCHARD: Why do you think that the only time that you should hit somebody is to defend yourself instead of trying to get even? Why is there a difference there for you?

EMILY: Because, why would you want [...] If you were mad at a person, then I could see why you would *want* to hit him, but that's no *reason* to hit a person.

CARLEN: I agree with Emily. When he bought him the ice cream cone, he was paying him back in a very nice way and not getting back at him, but just paying him back and doing something nice [...].

PENNY: I agree with those guys, too, because if you do something nice, and then you feel that, like, if somebody did something nice to me, then I'd feel bad if I didn't do something nice to them. So, I'd have to repay that back to them and that's kind of like-it's not getting even—but it's, well, it's just kind of [...].

CARLEN: Doing a favor.

PENNY: Yeah! Doing a favor and paying them back and getting even is a different kind of explanation.

Penny and Carlen had made an important distinction between repaying a favor and getting even. Both could be regarded as types of returning in kind, or paying back. But Penny and Carlen regard the latter as harmful and the former as beneficial. So, as Penny notes, they have "a different kind of explanation."

Larry next identified another type of returning in kind—but one which need not be construed as a type of paying back:

LARRY: I sort of agree with Emily, because, like, if some of our old neighbors here are having a bee-bee gun fight and they were out in the woods or something, and someone was back there, and they got hit by accident, and so they started throwing rocks because they were going to get shot at, and so they were only defending themselves.

Kurt then challenged the rather clean lines of analysis that had been proposed. What, he asked, counts as self-defense?

KURT: This is to Emily. What if they just kind of pick on you but you don't really need to defend yourself? What do you do there?

EMILY: What do you mean?

KURT: Well, like you said, you need to defend yourself. But you don't really need to defend yourself when they're just picking on you.

EMILY: I know. That's what I mean. Like, if somebody's hitting you and keeps on hitting you, and you try to run away, and they chase after you and start hitting you, I mean, that's when you need to defend yourself.

CHIP: Not when somebody is teasing you.

LARRY: But Kurt says, what do you do?

EMILY: Well, you just ignore him and walk away.

CHIP: Just the way they did it when the guy tripped him—you just walk [...]

LARRY: They didn't walk. They didn't walk. They ran.

KURT: Well, I just mean that not hitting each other, but just kind of poking you, kind of out of friendship; and she's just poking you, not hitting you or anything, and you don't run.

CHIP: Let's say—let's say if I hit Rick, and I go [he pats Rick's back], "Hey, Ricky" and he does it back to me or whatever. That's nothing unless they go—unless you're not buddies and you go like that and you hurt him. It wouldn't necessarily—you'd probably say, stop it, or something like that. I don't think you'd come up and say, "Hey you, hit me!" and punch him out in his face.

KURT: But Emily says you have to defend yourself on that. But you don't really need to.

EMILY: No, I'm saying you have to defend yourself when somebody keeps on hitting you and won't stop. [The discussion about whether ignoring the person who hits you will work continued, with several still concerned that the hitter will not always stop.]

CARLEN: Kurt, when he tricks you like that, you [...] just ignore him. You don't have to defend yourself, because it's just a little thing to get you—to get you mad. If he were to, like Emily said, chase after you and hit you or something like that, then you defend yourself. I mean, maybe then you've got to get him back. Not really get him back, but you have to defend yourself and hit him if he's hitting you.

PRITCHARD: We've been talking about kind of a special problem, where people are hitting each other. What if we change the example a little bit? Suppose that Harry and Timmy were walking along, and Timmy said, "Let's get an ice cream cone," and Harry said, "Yeah, that's a good idea." And they go into the store and Harry has money for the ice cream cone, but Timmy doesn't. And, in fact, Harry has enough money to pay for both, but Harry says, "Too bad you don't have enough money." Then Harry buys himself a cone and walks away [...] eating his cone while Timmy doesn't have one. What should happen there? Next time should Timmy do the same thing back? What do you think, Carlen?

CARLEN: I think that Timmy would be discouraged enough. But to get a good reputation and to maybe teach Harry to do it the next time, if Timmy had enough money to buy two cones and Harry didn't have any, to buy him one.

PRITCHARD: To teach him a lesson?

CARLEN: To teach him a lesson.

PRITCHARD: Is teaching someone a lesson different from trying to get even, or is that the same thing?

CARLEN: It's different, because [...] I think it's different.

PENNY: If you teach them a lesson, you're not going to hurt them, and if you get even, you're gonna hurt them.

PRITCHARD: Because you got hurt in the first place?

PENNY: Yeah.

Carlen's suggestion was one that had not been made before. Instead of returning in kind in the sense of literally doing the same thing to another, one could do to another what one would want the other to have done. This is a more hypothetical form of reciprocity. Why do this? Not to "get back" at someone. Rather, it would be to teach a lesson—a lesson in what would be desirable reciprocal behavior. Perhaps Penny is a bit optimistic in thinking that teaching someone a lesson will never hurt them, but her point gains plausibility if it is recast in terms of intent. [Although it should be acknowledged that, for some, sometimes "teaching a lesson" is scarcely distinguishable from "getting even."]

Since we were nearing the end of our session, I thought it would be good for us to try to pull our ideas together. I suggested that we try applying what they would recognize as the Golden Rule to the situations we had been discussing

PRITCHARD: What does what we call the Golden Rule mean when we talk about all these different examples? Does it mean different things in different situations?

PENNY: Like, if you think about what you're doing to people—if you want them to do it to you, how would you feel if they were doing it to you, and kind of saying, "Well, I wouldn't like that, so I won't do that to that person."

PRITCHARD: Even if they do it to you?

CHIP: That's what the rule would be. Do unto others as you want them to do unto you [...] .

CARLEN: I think that the rule would go to the ice cream cone if Harry were to buy Timmy one. Then Timmy would have to buy Harry one next time they go. I don't think it's the hit thing. I think that it shouldn't be there. I don't think that the rule is supposed to have you, when somebody hits you, to hit them back just to get them back.

EMILY: If you had money to buy two ice cream cones, and the other person you were with didn't have any money to buy an ice cream cone, and it would be just like vice versa. If the other kid had the money to buy two ice cream cones, then you would want him to buy you an ice cream cone. So you should buy the other kid an ice cream cone.

PRITCHARD: So what you're talking about is what you would want people to do to you and not what they actually do to you. [Larry then reopened the discussion of tactics—whether ignoring the person who hits you will work. Carlen continued to claim that ignoring might work.]

LARRY: But you were saying—you were saying that you should defend yourself also. So, if they hit me more than twice, I'm just going to belt them back.

CARLEN: Well, that's if they keep on hitting you and hitting you and you can't do anything. I would hit them back.

CHIP: I think both these things are sort of right. Okay, now, if someone comes up and he attacks you and everything and he hits you and everything, then you can ignore them. But if it doesn't work, then you have to go to something else. But you can ignore them also, Larry, and then if it doesn't work and someone comes up and belts you, then you have to do something [...].

RICK: But if [...] you're thinking they'll pay you back or something, and you go out and buy an ice cream cone, or whatever, you gotta take the chance that maybe they won't pay you back. Like, they could say, "Oh. Oh, this must be the cone you owed me three years ago. I'm glad you paid it back. Now get lost, boy. Thanks." And he just may never pay you back.

PRITCHARD: So, does that mean that we should be cautious when we are going to do favors?

CHIP: Uh, huh!

PRITCHARD: Because you don't know? Would you do someone a favor only if you thought they would return it later?

GROUP: [Mixed response: Yeah, no, no, no, no [...].]

LARRY: You shouldn't always expect someone to return your favors.

RICK: You should try to give, not receive.

PRITCHARD: If someone does you a favor, do you think that you should always do something nice for them? [Group: Yeah, yeah, yeah [...].]

CARLEN: If it's a favor. If it's a favor, then you want to do it, do something
back to them and pay up for them for what they did, and do it to
them also; but if it was just a hit or something, you don't want to do it.

PRITCHARD: How about if someone thinks they're doing you a favor,
but it's something that you really don't want? But you know they're
trying to do you a favor?

CARLEN: You should accept it as a favor.

PRITCHARD: And then do something nice for them?

RICK: Try to just give. You don't need to receive all the time, because if
you just give [...] and others are in the giving mood, you don't have
to worry about not receiving something, because everybody's going
to feel the same way. They feel a lot better to give, but they know
that everybody else will be giving, and they'll receive still.

Rather than focus on specific exchanges of favors, Rick brought the group's
attention to the general practice of doing favors. Although it is unlikely that all
will benefit alike from the widespread practice of doing favors, Rick had astutely
pointed out that favors need not come from those to whom one has extended
favors. Thus, from a more general perspective, the practice of doing favors
even for those from whom one has not received (nor ever will) has much to
commend it. This could be thought of as a form of indirect reciprocity.

We were signaled that the videotaping of the session was ending. The
cameras receded, and the lights dimmed. But our group carried on for
several minutes. They had performed well before the cameras. But obviously,
they were not merely performing for cameras or their viewers. They had not
finished working through the issues at hand—together.

This concluded the philosophical sessions I had with this group while they
were 5th graders. These sessions had all illustrated features of conversation
that Smith would agree encourage the sort of reasonableness that he held in
such high regard. Admittedly Smith would not have witnessed anything quite
like this in his moral philosophy classes at Glasgow. Although many of his
students were teenagers they were not as young as these 5th graders, and his
lecture format did not invite his students to take the lead in discussions. Would
he have applauded IAPC's efforts to create classrooms as communities of
inquiry had he witnessed them? Given the standard pedagogical techniques
of his day, he might have been somewhat skeptical. But this does not mean
that those who today support the inclusion of philosophical reflection in
K-12 curricula cannot incorporate Smith's ideas about conversation and
reasonableness in their classes.

As good fortune would have it, my group of 5th graders retained their
enthusiasm for philosophical enquiry. Two years after they had their series

of after-school sessions as 5th graders, the group requested that we have a "reunion" in the Ransom Public Library. I need not have worried about initiating topics for discussion. We quickly found ourselves returning to some of the mind/brain issues that they had argued about so vigorously during several of our previous sessions. Once again, no consensus emerged. Four years after this, when they were nearing the end of the 11th grade, I received a letter from two members of the group. Now, 11th graders, Emily and Carlen wrote that they were certain that they had been right all along about the relationship between the brain and the mind. They included an article from the local paper that contended that the mind is best understood in terms of the make-up and functioning of the brain. They suggested that our group meet one more time, this time to talk about whether this article succeeded in making its case. We met but, predictably, no consensus on the topic at hand was reached. Finally, as he had frequently done in the past, Jeff pressed me, "What's the answer, Dr. Pritchard. Tell us what the answer is!" Once again, I urged Jeff and the others that they needed to take responsibility for developing and defending their own positions rather than simply defer to what they thought mine might be. Others agreed. However, they added, they were disappointed that such critical thinking was not encouraged in their high school classes.

In late 2017, a full three decades after I had last had contact with anyone in the group, I was surprised (and delighted) to receive an email from Emily. She reported that she and Rick had recently been exchanging emails about how special their after-school philosophical adventures in the Ransom Public Library had been. It was, they agreed, truly unique and memorable. Emily mentioned that she now had a preteen daughter of her own who exhibited much philosophical curiosity. So, I sent them a copy of *Hey Who, Who Are You?*, a fictional story I had recently written.[2] Hey Who, a curious little owl, puzzled over questions about his identity. For example, how do we, unlike most other species, come to recognize that we are looking at *ourselves* when gazing at a mirror? To the very end, Hey Who remains skeptical, offering formidable arguments that he and the owl he is looking at in the pond in front of him cannot be one and the same owl.. The story ends with Hey Who still puzzled about claims to the contrary, but eager to continue exploring questions about who he is. Emily reported that her daughter now shared Hey Who's enthusiasm for such questions. Emily said that they had also begun vigorously exchanging ideas about relationships between the brain and mind—a philosophical topic that apparently continued to fascinate Emily so many years after our after-school library group came under its grip.

---

2 Buttonwood Press: Haslett, Michigan, 2017.

CONCLUDING THOUGHTS

Previous chapters in this monograph have shown that Adam Smith and Thomas Reid commented extensively and favorably on Joseph Butler's earlier analysis of the importance of resentment and forgiveness in the moral development of children. All three philosophers emphasize that the interplay of sentiment and reason is fundamental. David Hume, too, admired the work of Butler. However, although he was familiar with their writings on these topics, Hume had little to say about resentment and forgiveness.

As noted earlier, Glen Pettigrove, current holder of Glasgow University's Chair of Moral Philosophy, offers an account of how meekness was commonly regarded in eighteenth-century Scotland that might help explain Hume's apparent silence about Butler's views on these matters. Meekness was seen as a virtuous disposition marked by slowness to anger, but not moral submissiveness. Also, as Pettigrew points out, some sort of training is involved in its acquisition. Had Hume acknowledged this and discussed key factors this involves, differences among Hume, Smith, and Reid regarding the roles of sentiment and reason in moral development would likely be seen as less extreme.

Assessed by the criteria of reasonableness advanced by Butler, Smith, Reid, and Hume (at least in the opening chapter of his *Enquiry Concerning the Principles of Morals*), today's public discourse does not fare very well. It is all too often dominated by one-sided, bold advocacy of one's point of view and weakly supported derision of those who dare to dissent, thus displaying a serious moral failure to consider issues fully and fairly. This would no doubt be a great disappointment to pragmatist John Dewey (1859–1952) were he here to observe the quality of public discourse among adults on vital social and political issues facing us today. More than a century ago in his *Reconstruction of Philosophy*, Dewey offered advice as sound now as it was then[1]:

> Morals is not a catalogue of acts nor a set of rules to be applied like drugstore prescriptions or cook-book recipes. The need in morals is for

---

1 In *John Dewey: The Middle Works, 1899–1924*, vol. 12, ed. Jo Ann Boydston (Carbondale: Southern Illinois University Press, 1991), p. 177. Cited in James D. Wallace, *Ethical Norms, Particular Cases* (Ithaca, NY: Cornell University Press, 1996), p. 43.

specific methods of inquiry and contrivance: Methods of inquiry to locate difficulties and evils; methods of contrivance to form plans to be used as working hypotheses in dealing with them. And the pragmatic import of the logic of individualized situations, each having its own irreplaceable good and principle, is to transfer the attention of theory from preoccupation with general conceptions to the problem of developing effective methods of inquiry.

Dewey's view was that the task of assisting children in developing effective methods of moral inquiry should not wait until they have nearly become adults. In the last few decades of the twentieth century, a variety of popular educational efforts made their way into K-12 educational settings. One such effort was made by advocates of "values clarification."[2] However, this was met with the charge of relativism, as values were only supposed to be clarified, not critically evaluated. This could not satisfy Dewey's desire for "effective methods of inquiry" that require methods of reflection, imagination, and good judgment. This, in turn, calls for the development of appropriate virtues, or habits of mind.

It might be thought that Dewey would have welcomed the revival of programs on virtues and character education in the schools that succeeded the "values clarification" approach. However, promising as programs on virtues and character could be, some of the more popular ones implemented in schools fall far short of what Dewey called for. Broadly cast as their proposed lists of virtues are, they omit one that Dewey would recognize as fundamental: *reasonableness*. Such programs do not seem to recognize the need to learn ways of resolving possible conflicts among the listed virtues themselves. Instead, they simply set aside a special time in the school day to focus primarily on reciting their list of moral virtues.

However, rather than seeing virtue and character education as a separable recitation session, with Dewey we might see it best as an *aspect*, or *dimension*, of any standard subject area. So, the study of history could include careful reflection on the moral dimensions of history—of laws, slavery, the treatment of women, the forcible removal of native peoples from their land, wars, as well as of moral advancements. The study of literature could include explicit attention to, and critical reflection on, moral themes running through poetry, short stories, and novels. The study of science could include

---

2 For a critical discussion of the content and shortcomings of the values clarification movement, see William L. Ryan, "Incoherence and Contradiction in the Values Clarification Movement," *McGill Journal of Education*, Vol. 24, No. 2, Spring 1989, pp. 173–186.

the moral dimensions of scientific research, as well as environmental moral challenges. But, to satisfy Dewey, careful study of the moral dimensions of these standard subjects must emphasize the importance of promoting "effective methods of inquiry."

Helping children develop such methods of inquiry requires respecting their abilities as moral inquirers from the outset. This includes respecting their moral and philosophical interests and abilities. By the time children first enter school, they are already somewhat sophisticated moral inquirers, with strong ideas about what is fair and unfair, kind and cruel, honest and dishonest, and so on. At the same time, their reflections on such matters need to be much further developed, refined, and applied to new challenges.

Recent work supported by the John Templeton Foundation and the Kern Family Foundation would likely receive Dewey's approval. The Jubilee Centre for Character and Virtues in Birmingham, England receives funding from both and annually hosts an international conference that emphasizes critical thinking and moral judgment in virtue and character education.[3]

Prior to the emergence of the Jubilee Centre's efforts, kindergarten teacher Vivian Gussin Paley (1929–2019) was celebrated for being especially adept at promoting reflective inquiry with young children.[4] Recipient of the prestigious MacArthur Fellowship in 1989, Paley not only wrote and discussed (with children and adults) stories for children, but she also wrote about her experiences as a teacher. For example, her *You Can't Say You Can't Play* (Harvard University Press, 1992) recounts discussions she had about fairness, respect, kindness, and rules with kindergarten through 5th-grade children. These discussions all pivot around the question of whether there should be a rule about children playing together at school: "You Can't Say You Can't Play." Her inquiry was prompted by a problem she encountered as a teacher: What should be done about the harms suffered by children in her classrooms who are excluded from joining others in play—that is, children who see themselves as rejected?

Paley discussed the suggested rule with her kindergarten class for several months before actually implementing it with them. But even then the problems

---

3 PLATO, IAPC, and ICPIC, all of which have websites, also are organizations strongly supportive of including critical thinking in moral education programs for children that they feature. See my Stanford Encyclopedia of Philosophy (SEP) entry, "Philosophy for Children" (4th ed., 2022) for some discussion of these and other resources.

4 This discussion of Vivian Paley's ideas is based on pp. 23–25 of my "Moral Philosophy for Children and Character Education," in *International Journal of Applied Philosophy*, Vol. 14, No. 1, 13–26, Spring 2000.

the rule addresses were not completely resolved. She also discussed these problems with older children and learned more about the need to keep trying to refine the rule.

She concluded that it is important to continue such efforts because of what is at stake and because this can stimulate thoughtful discussion of the wider issues. As Paley put it, "You Can't Say You Can't Play" is a different kind of rule than those forbidding hitting or the destruction of property. These rules are viewed as basically necessary and uncontroversial. Her suggested rule, however, goes against practices that are widely viewed as a normal part of social life. We choose to do things with our friends that exclude others. Small groups of children gather to play with each other. Others are left out. Some groups may operate with a "boss rule," which involves one or two children deciding for the group who will or will not be allowed to join.

However, Paley asked, what do these exclusionary practices do to those who are excluded? How do they feel? When she invited students to discuss these questions, she was barraged with stories of the disappointment and pain of being rejected. Virtually all the children, regardless of grade level, had vivid, detailed experiences to relate—experiences both in their classrooms and school recess activities.

Paley then asked two questions about the rule "You Can't Say You Can't Play." First, is it *fair*? Second, will it *work*? An interesting, and important, feature of Paley's exploration of these questions with the children is that she was as uncertain about what the best answers are as the children were. Although most agreed that the rule is fair, it is clear that they had serious concerns about moral costs that might come with the rule. After all, friendship is limited, and don't friends have some right to be together in ways that exclude others? What if someone insists on playing but ruins the play by being uncooperative or disruptive? And what about *forcing* people to play with those they don't want to play with? These questions, and many others, were raised and carefully discussed by the children, kindergarten through fifth grade.

Paley respected the ability of even kindergartners to reflect on the rules governing their lives in school. Thus, she embarked on what was essentially a practical philosophical journey with the students. Furthermore, this journey was as much hers as the children's.

Paley's exemplary work illustrates the promise of it being a *shared* search undertaken by teachers and students together.

So, although there can be shared agreement that trustworthiness, respect, responsibility, fairness, caring, and citizenship constitute basic virtues that warrant support and careful attention in the schools, Vivian Paley's efforts serve as a model of inquiry that allows reasonableness to be given pride of place in the education of children as they reflect on moral problems they are facing now. This encourages them to continue to do so as they encounter new kinds of problems as their future unfolds.

Of course, some parents, teachers, and other adults may fear that taking these views seriously will interfere with their responsibility to help shape the future of children. However, as philosopher R.M. Hare pointed out long ago, children must learn to cope with many voices, not only those of parents, religious leaders, and teachers but also those of peers, the media and entertainment world, and the rest of our diverse and challenging world. At some point, children need to be well equipped critically to evaluate the welter of messages bombarding them. Hare concludes[5]:

> We have got to try to fit [children] to make, *for themselves*, the choices with which they will inevitably be faced. And these will be choices, not just of hair-styles, but of some of the most fundamental elements in their ways of life. Furthermore, whatever the schools do or do not include in their curricula, children will be exposed elsewhere to ideas that can challenge their beliefs in unsettling ways. Given this, encouraging philosophical reflection in children is better regarded as an ally rather than a foe—both by children themselves and those who want them to become responsible and reasonable adults.

Such reflection encourages children to become more fully aware of the significance of being able to articulate and commit themselves to values that emphasize the importance of dispositions that subscribe to their being able to join with others in reasonable conversation and action—even in the face of substantial disagreement.

How the schools might best encourage this sort of critical conversation is a matter of crucial importance—and controversy. Fortunately, as the Jubilee Centre and others illustrate, recently there has been a significant growth in solid research on this topic by researchers. Unfortunately, despite this, communication among researchers from diverse areas may still reflect the continued tendency of institutions of higher learning to support the rather "siloed" approach to disciplinary work that emerged in the twentieth century.

Consider the insightful *The Case for Contention: Teaching Controversial Issues in American Schools*, edited by Jonathan Zimmerman and Emily Robertson (University of Chicago Press, 2017). The contributors analyze ways of encouraging classroom discussions of controversial issues that employ the use of standards of reasonableness in the exchange of ideas. However, although there is occasional

---

5 Hare, R M., *Essays in Religion and Education* (Oxford: Clarendon Press, 1992), p. 140.

reference to John Dewey, the contributors do not discuss the influence of eighteenth-century Scottish thinkers on earlier American educational programs in the schools. For example, Dugald Stewart (1753–1828), a devoted student of both Smith and Reid, was admired by educators of his day in both Europe and the early years of the United States for his detailed support of the reflective abilities of children.[6] There is also no mention of any of the increasing efforts of various organizations over the past half-century to develop programs for the schools that explicitly promote the philosophical thinking of children.[7]

Another especially noteworthy recent book advocating the linking of critical thinking and moral commitment in the schools is *Teaching Controversial Issues: The Case for Critical Thinking and Moral Commitment in the Classroom*, edited by Nel Noddings and Laurie Brooks (New York: Teachers College Press, 2017). Although this book makes strong use of relevant philosophical literature (including Dewey's), it refers only to Hume among eighteenth-century Scottish philosophers. Also, like the Zimmerman and Robertson book, it does not mention Matthews, Lipman, Sharp, or others active in recent efforts to join children and adults in the world of philosophical reflection.

So, it would seem, there is ample room for critical discussion among philosophers, moral psychologists, and educators who are evaluating programs in the schools that support advancing the reasonableness of children. On the one hand, for example, already mentioned above in Chapter 3 are the challenges that Virgil Henry Storr and Henrietta John pose for Adam Smith's reliance on the idea of an "impartial spectator." On the other hand, there is Fiachra Long's "Thomas Reid and Philosophy with Children," *Journal of Philosophy of Education*, 39, pp. 599–614 (2005), a detailed account of Reid's understanding of philosophical curiosity and its exemplification in children. Such discussions offer helpful contributions to our understanding of what is needed in advancing the reasonableness of children as they mature. My hope is that this monograph also makes some useful contributions in this direction.

---

6 For more on Stewart see my "Dugald Stewart" in *The International Encyclopedia of Ethics*, 1st ed., edited by Hugh LaFollette, Blackwell Publishing Ltd, entry #726, pp. 1–6 (2013).

7 For a discussion of many of these efforts, see my online, "Philosophy for Children" (4th ed. 2022), *Stanford Encyclopedia of Philosophy*. http://plato.stanford.edu/entries/children/.

BIBLIOGRAPHY

Benjamin, Martin. *Splitting the Difference: Compromise and Integrity in Ethics and Politics* (Lawrence, KS: University Press of Kansas, 1991).

Butler, Joseph. *Fifteen Sermons*, T.A. Roberts, ed. (London: Society for Promoting Christian Knowledge, 1970).

Dewey, John. *John Dewey: The Middle Works, 1899–1924*, vol. 12, Jo Ann Boydston, ed. (Carbondale: Southern Illinois University Press, 1991).

Englehardt, Elaine E. and Michael S. Pritchard, "18th Century Scottish Philosophers and Children," presented at the 2017 International Council for Philosophical Inquiry with Children (ICPIC) program in Madrid, Spain.

Gert, Bernard. *Common Morality* (Oxford, 2004).

Gopnik, Allison. *The Scientist in the Crib* (William Morrow, 1999).

Gopnik, Allison. *The Philosophical Baby* (NY: Farrar, Straus, and Giroux, 2009).

Gregory, Maughn and Megan Laverty, eds., *Community of Inquiry with Ann Margaret Sharp* (NY: Routledge, 2019).

Gregory, Maughn and Megan Laverty, eds., *Gareth B. Matthews, The Child's Philosopher* (NY: Routledge, 2022).

Hare, R M., *Essays in Religion and Education* (Oxford: Clarendon Press, 1992).

Hoffman, Martin. *Empathy and Moral Development* (Barnes & Noble, 2000).

Hume, David. *An Enquiry Concerning the Principles of Morals*, Tom L. Beauchamp, eds. (Oxford, 1998).

Hume, David. *Four Dissertations* (London: A. Millar in the Strand, 1757).

Lipman, Matthew. *Harry Stottlemeier's Discovery* (Montclair State University, Institute for the Advancement of Children, 1970).

Matthews, Gareth. *Philosophy and the Young Child* (Harvard, 1980).

Matthews, Gareth. *Dialogues with Children* (Harvard, 1984).

Noddings, Nel and Laurie Brooks, eds. *Teaching Controversial Issues: The Case for Critical Thinking and Moral Commitment in the Classroom* (New York: Teachers College Press, 2017).

Paley, Vivian. *You Can't Say You Can't Play* (Harvard University Press, 1992).

Pettigrove, Glen, "Meekness and 'Moral' Anger" (*Ethics*, Jan. 2012).

Plato. *Five Dialogues*. Trans. By G.M.A. Grube (Indianapolis: Hackett Publishers, 1981).

Pritchard, Michael S., *Reasonable Children* (University Press of Kansas, 1996).

Pritchard, Michael S., "Philosophy for Children" (online in the *Stanford Encyclopedia of Philosophy, 2022*).

Pritchard, Michael S., *Philosophical Adventures with Children* (University Press of America, 1985).

Pritchard, Michael S., *Hey Who, Who Are You?* (Buttonwood Press: Haslett, MI, 2017).

Pritchard, Michael S., "Sidgwick's *Practical Ethics*," *International Journal of Applied Philosophy*, 12:2, 1998, 147–151.

Pritchard, Michael S. "Justice and Resentment in Hume, Smith, and Reid," *Journal of Scottish Philosophy*, 6:1, 2008, 59–70.

Pritchard, Michael S., "Thomas Reid on the 'Seeds of Morality'," *The Journal of Scottish Thought*, 4, 2011, 1–15.

Pritchard, Michael S., "Taming Resentment," in *New Essays on Adam Smith's Moral Philosophy*, Wade L. Robison and David B. Suits, eds. (Rochester, NY: RIT Press, 2012).

Reed, Ronald and Ann M. Sharp, eds., *Studies in Philosophy for Children: Harry Stottlemeier's Discovery* (Philadelphia: Temple University Press, 1992).

Reid, Thomas, *Essays on the Active Powers of Man*, First published in 1788, but subsequently edited by Knud Haakonessen and James A. Harris (Edinburgh University Press, 2010).

Ryan, William. "Incoherence and Contradiction in the Values Clarification Movement," *McGill Journal of Education*, 24:2, Spring 1989, pp. 173–186.

Sibley, W.M., "The Rational Versus the Reasonable," *Philosophical Review*, 62, 1953, pp. 554–560.

Sidgwick, Henry. *Practical Ethics*, Introduction by Sissela Bok (New York: Oxford University Press, 1998).

Sidgwick, Henry. *The Methods of Ethics*, 7th ed., originally published in 1907 (London: MacMillan & Co. Limited 1963).

Smith, Adam. *The Theory of Moral Sentiments*, D.D. Raphael and A.L. Macfie, eds. (Indianapolis: Liberty Fund, Inc., 1984). The original 6th edition was published in 1790.

Splitter, Laurence J. and Ann M. Sharp, *Teaching Better Thinking: The Classroom Community of Inquiry* (Melbourne: Australian Center for Educational Research, 1995).

Storr, Virgil and Henrietta John, "The Impersonal Spectator's Cultural Spectacles," in *Of Sympathy and Selfishness*, C.S. Thomas, ed. (Mercer University Press, 2015).

Wallace, James D. *Ethical Norms, Particular Cases* (Ithaca, NY: Cornell University Press, 1996).

Zimmerman, Jonathan and Emily Robertson, eds., *The Case for Contention: Teaching Controversial Issues in American Schools* (University of Chicago Press, 2017).

INDEX

9 781839 986277